T0019960

Complete
KINDERGARTEN
MATH
Workbook

175 Fun Activities to Build Math, Logic, and Critical Thinking Skills

Naoya Imanishi, MEd

Illustrated by Gareth Williams

A **Brightly** Book

Z KIDS · NEW YORK

Copyright © 2022 by Penguin Random House LLC

All rights reserved.

Published in the United States by Z Kids, an imprint of Zeitgeist™,
a division of Penguin Random House LLC, New York.
penguinrandomhouse.com

Zeitgeist™ is a trademark of Penguin Random House LLC
ISBN: 9780593435496

Illustrations by Gareth Williams
Author photo © by Jennifer Lazaro
Book design by Katy Brown
Edited by Meg Ilasco

Printed in the United States of America
3 5 7 9 10 8 6 4 2

First Edition

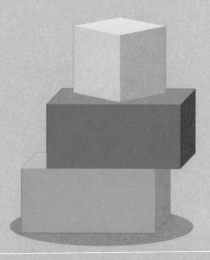

CONTENTS

INTRODUCTION · 5

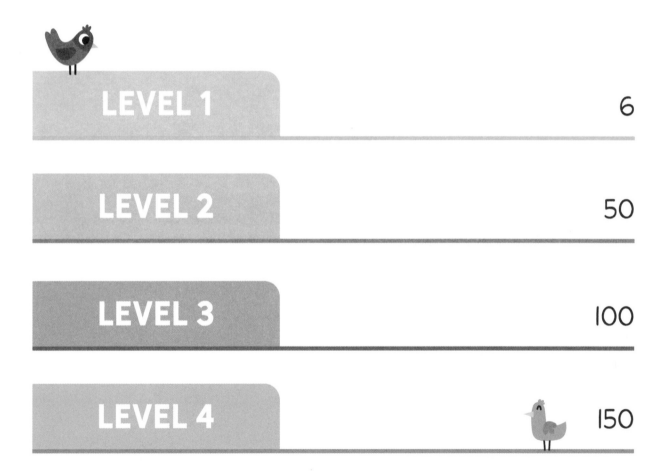

$$1 + 2 = 3$$

$$2 + 2 = 4$$

$$3 + 2 = 5$$

INTRODUCTION

HELLO! Welcome to the exciting world of kindergarten math. This book is a fun resource designed to engage your child through puzzles, games, word problems, and number sense activities. Every page is designed to keep your child entertained while developing math, logic, and critical thinking skills aligned with kindergarten curriculum.

As an educator for over 20 years, I have enjoyed developing math lessons to help children succeed. I have worked as an elementary school teacher and a math coach, as well as a facilitator of Cognitively Guided Instruction with the UCLA Mathematics Project.

This book is organized by levels. You will notice a progression of skills at each level that will increase your child's confidence and conceptual understanding. Your child may need assistance in reading the instructions or help in understanding concepts, and that's okay. Make sure to allow for some time to help them think it through, and if they are experiencing any frustration, you can always skip the activity and return to it later. The Common Core State Standards for Mathematical Practice address perseverance and justifying one's thinking. It's okay to let your child struggle through a problem. Allow them to progress at their own pace, but ask questions along the way. Engage their thinking by asking, "How did you know that?" or "I see how you got that number, is there another way to get that solution?"

I hope you enjoy watching your child have fun as they learn math and beam with pride as they progress through the book!

Naoya Imanishi, MEd

Activity 1

COUNTING FUN

How many objects are there? Circle the number.

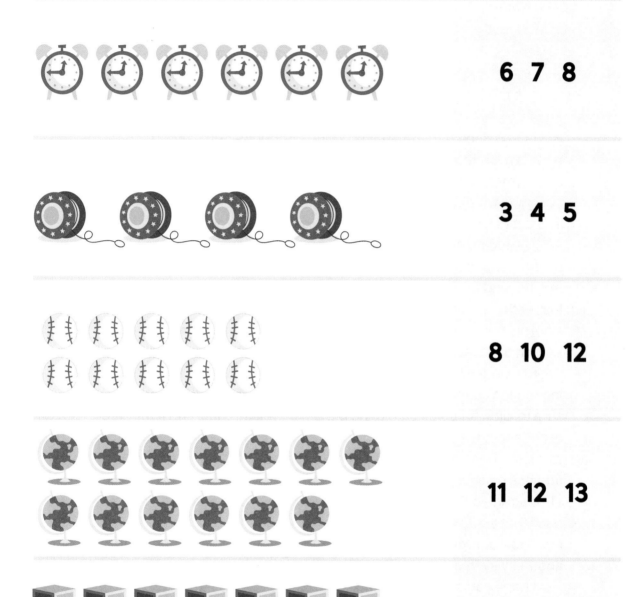

6 7 8

3 4 5

8 10 12

11 12 13

14 15 16

FOLLOW THE TRAIN

Connect the dots from 1 to 20 and hop aboard the Number Express!

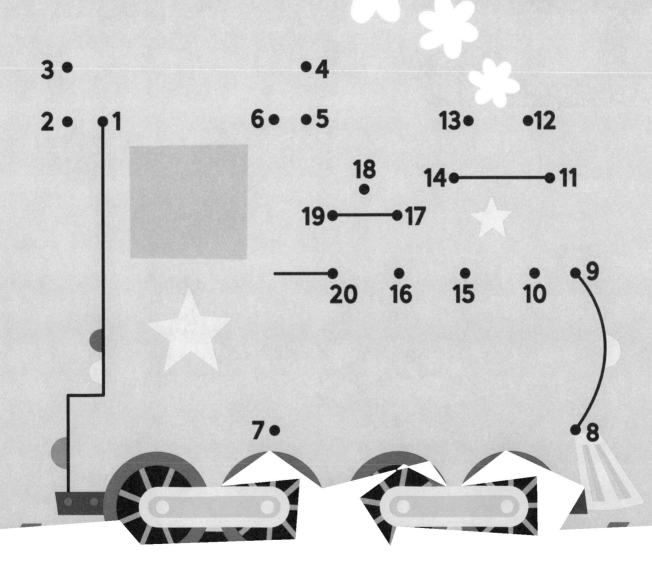

Activity 3

NUMBER HUNT

Circle the numbers 1 to 20 hidden in the kitchen. Can you find them all? Check off each one you find.

1	2	3	4	5	6	7	8	9	10
11	12	13	14	15	16	17	18	19	20

Activity 4

UNDER THE SEA

Count each group and write the number.

_____	_____	_____	_____	_____

Activity 5

COUNT IT

How many flowers are there? Write the number.

SCORE

Count the balls and write the number on the scoreboard.

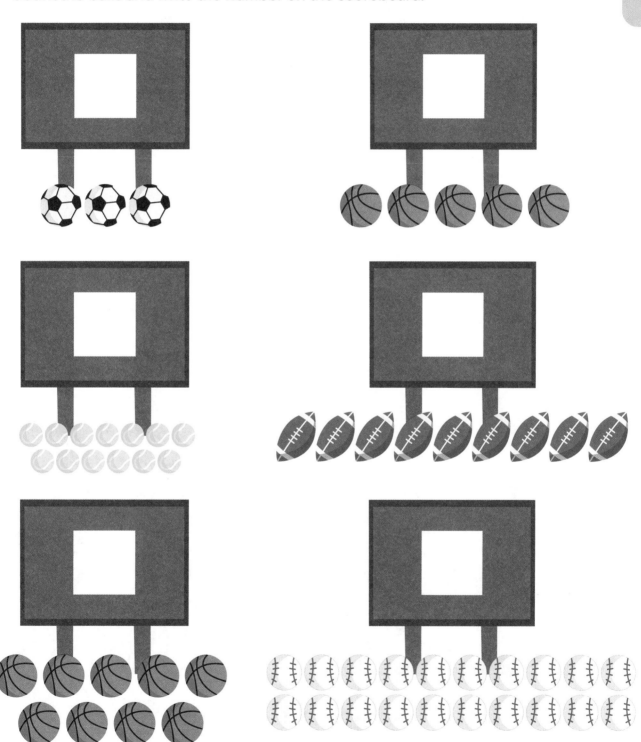

Activity 7

SUPERSTARS

Circle the group of stars that matches the number.

8

6

5

14

19

NUMBERS AND WORDS

Draw a line to match the number and its word.

1	THREE
2	SEVEN
3	NINE
4	FOUR
5	EIGHT
6	FIVE
7	ONE
8	TEN
9	TWO
10	SIX

Activity 9

NUMBER NAME DETECTIVE

For each number word, color in the same number of nearby objects.

FIVE

ONE

NINE

EIGHT

TWO

SIX

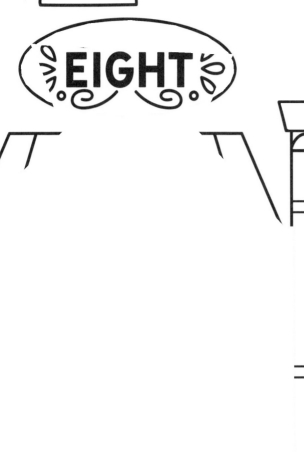

Activity 10

MATCH UP

Trace the word, then draw a line from the word to the number.

sixteen   **20**

eleven   **15**

twenty   **12**

fifteen   **18**

nineteen   **11**

thirteen   **13**

eighteen   **16**

twelve   **19**

WHAT'S THE WORD?

Complete the crossword puzzle! Use clues to help you fill in the number names.

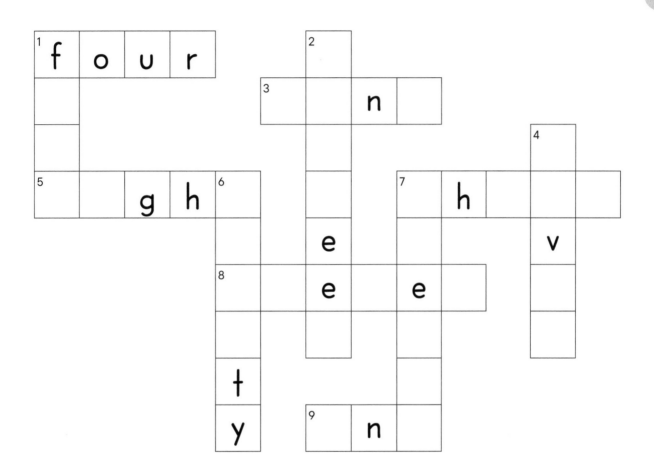

ACROSS →

1.

3.

5.

7.

8.

9.

DOWN ↓

1.

2.

4.

6.

7.

Activity 12

I SEE ICE CREAM

How many scoops of each ice cream flavor are there?
Write the number.

___   ___   ___   ___   ___

Activity 13
PUPPY PLAYTIME

How many bones are in each group? Write the number.

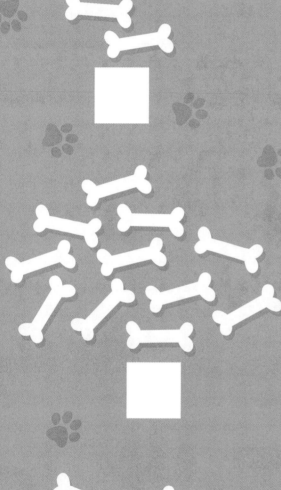

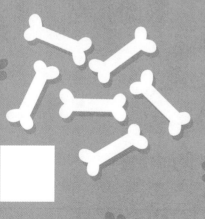

Activity 14

GROCERY SHOPPING

How many of each grocery item can you find? Write the number.

FRESH FOOD

APPLES

BREAD

_____   _____   _____   _____   _____

Activity 15

GARDEN MAZE

Find your way through the garden following the path in order from 1 to 20.

Activity 16

COUNT THE DOTS

How many dots are in the ten frames? Write the number.

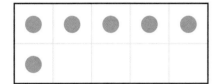 _____

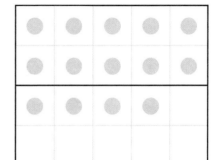 _____

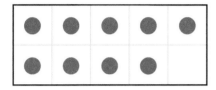 _____

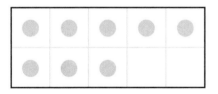 _____

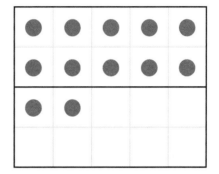 _____

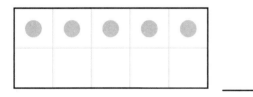 _____

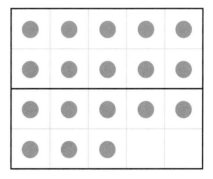 _____

Activity 17

SORT THE STUFF

Which group does each item belong in? Draw a line from each picture to the correct group.

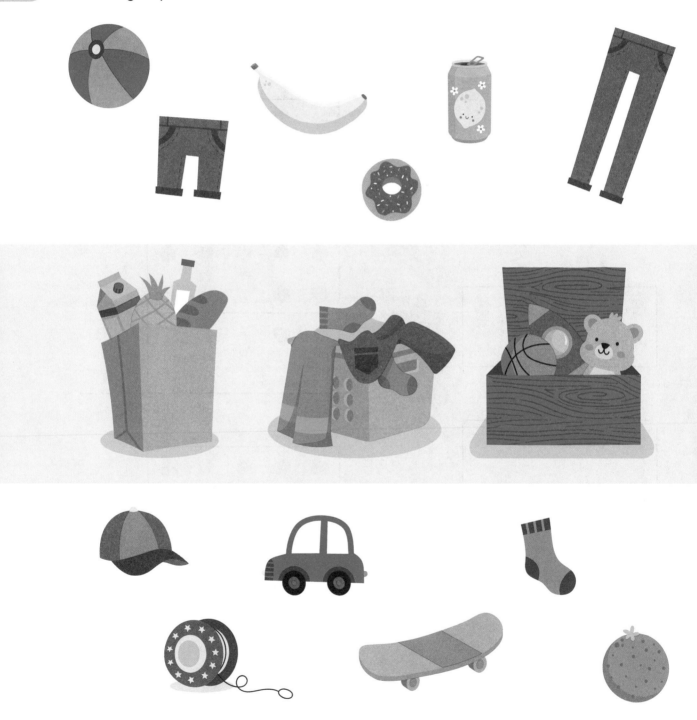

FEELING SPORTY

How many of each ball are there? Write the number.

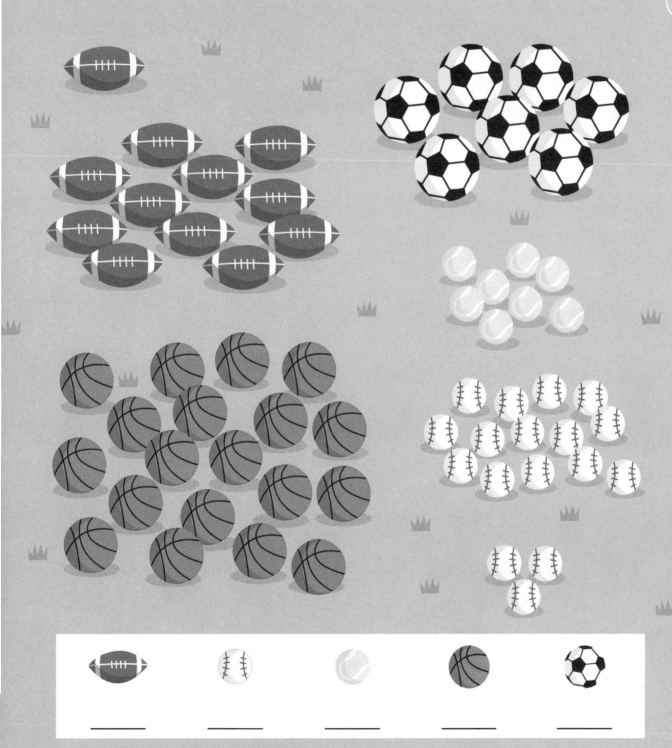

_____   _____   _____   _____   _____

Activity 19

HOW MANY STARS?

Circle a group of stars and write the number next to it.

(Note to parents: Let your child choose any cluster that makes sense to them.)

FIND FIVE

On each island, circle 5 animals.

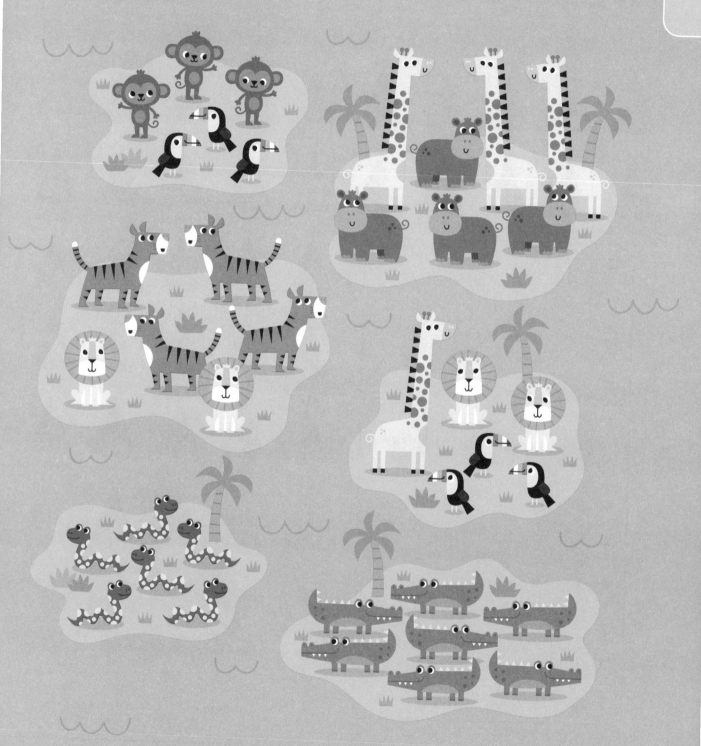

Activity 21

PARTY HATS

With a matching crayon, color a space on the graph for each type of hat.

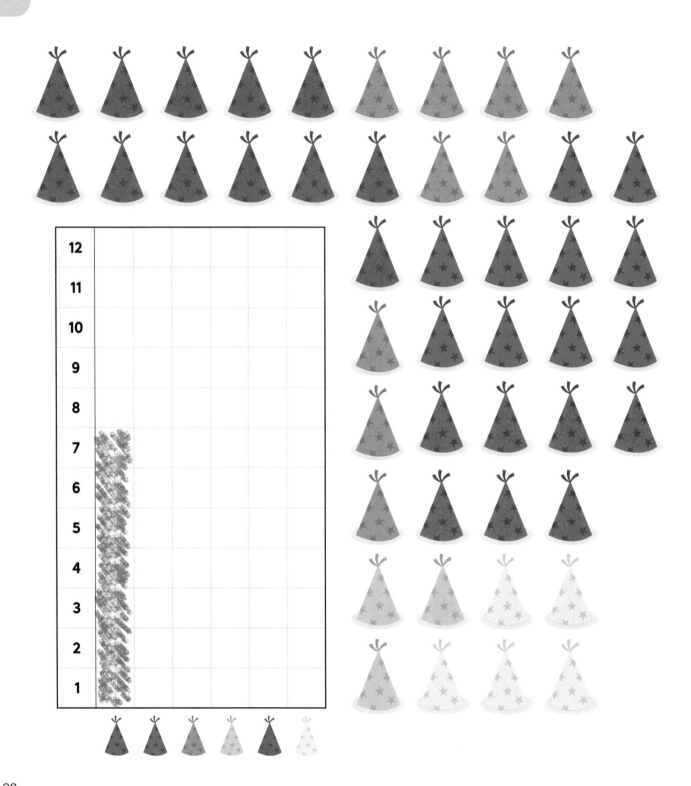

MATCH THE PIGGIES

Draw a line to match the number with the correct tally marks.

Activity 23

PERFECT PET SHOP

Count the number of each pet and and tally up your answers.

BUSY FARM

In each set, circle the group that has MORE animals.

Activity 25

BOBA FUN

In each set, circle the cup that has MORE boba balls.

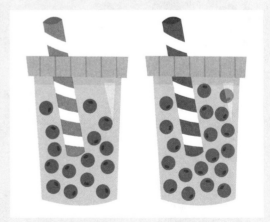

Activity 26
ALL ABOARD

Which has LESS? In each set, circle the train car that has FEWER passengers.

Activity 27

FIND THE SAME

Circle the two sets of cages that have the same number of birds in each cage.

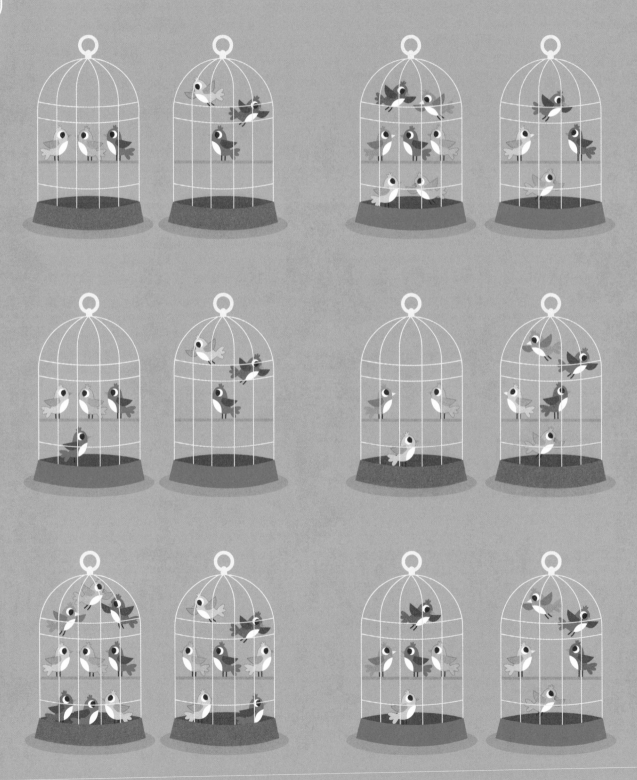

Activity 28

MAGIC HOUR

Which has the LEAST? In each set, color that card with the FEWEST amount of shapes.

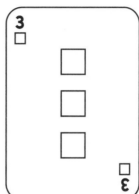

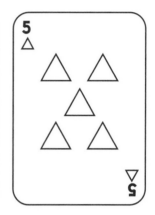

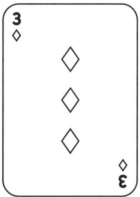

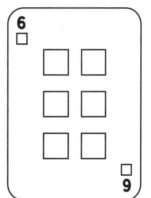

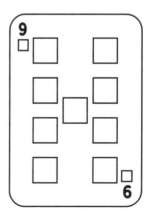

35

Activity 29
SHIP SHAPE

Count the hidden shapes on the pirate ship. How many of each can you find? Write the number.

CORNERS AND SIDES

Trace the sides of each shape and circle the corners.

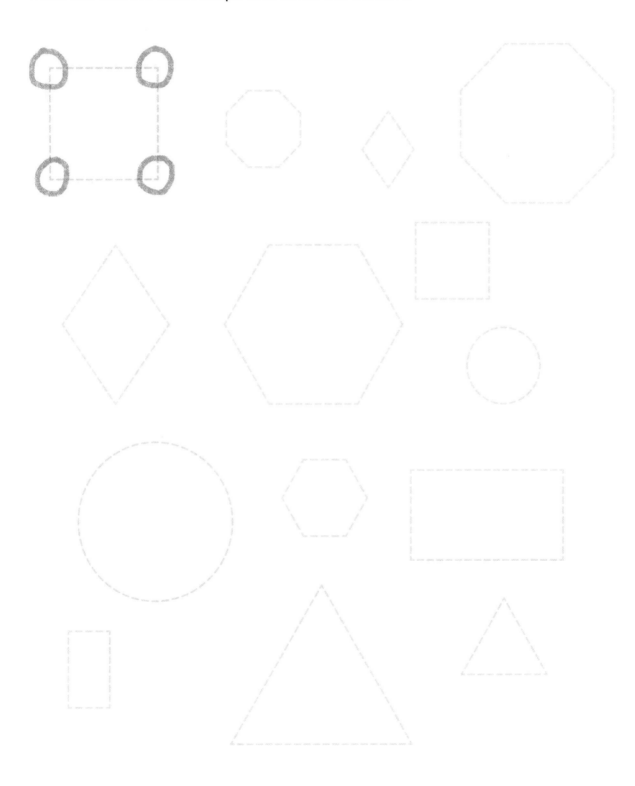

37

Activity 31

SHAPE UP

Complete the drawings by adding shapes.

SHAPES INSIDE

You can make shapes using other shapes! Using different crayons, trace the outline and color each shape.

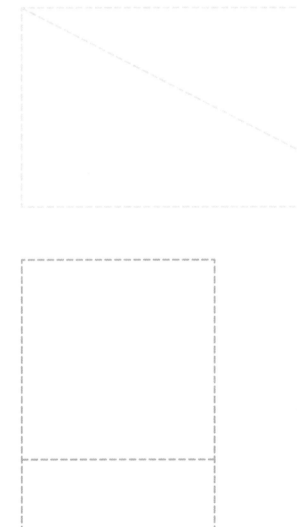

Activity 33

COMPARING CORNERS

Count the corners of the shapes in each set. Circle the shape that has MORE corners.

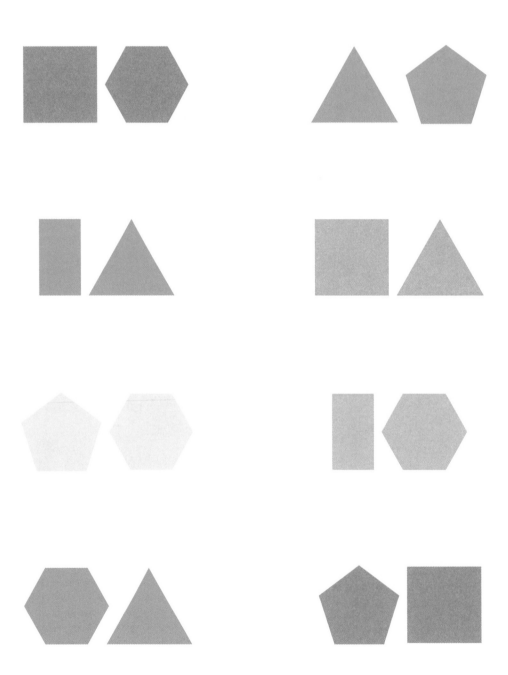

Activity 34

CITY SHAPES

Find and color the shapes using the color key.

Activity 35

BOWLING FUN

Count the pins and fill in the missing number to add up to 10.

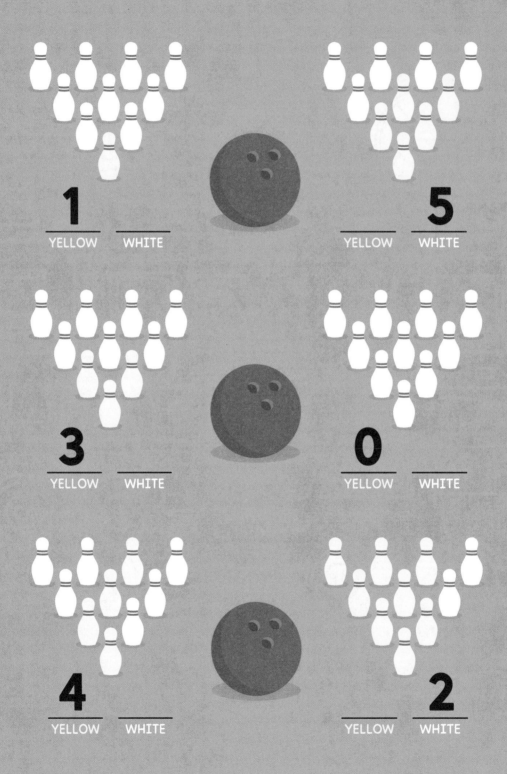

1 ___
YELLOW   WHITE

___ **5**
YELLOW   WHITE

3 ___
YELLOW   WHITE

0 ___
YELLOW   WHITE

4 ___
YELLOW   WHITE

___ **2**
YELLOW   WHITE

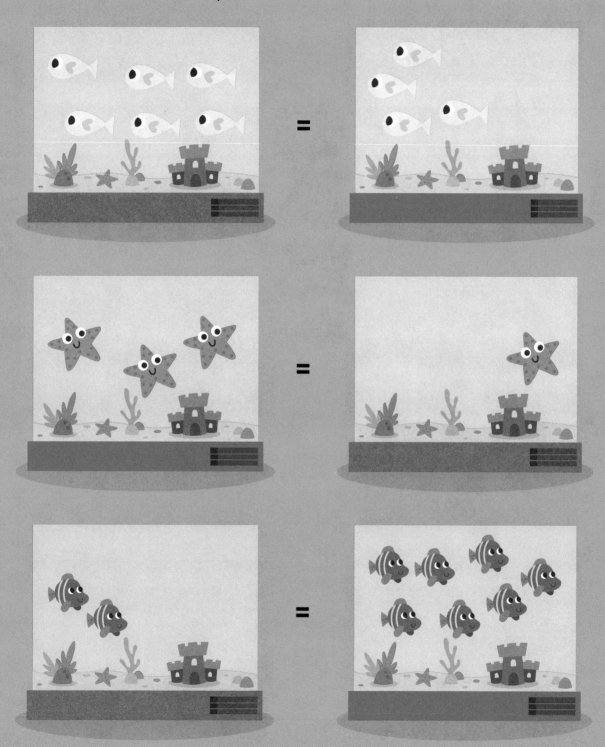

Activity 36

AQUARIUM LIFE

Count the sea creatures in each tank, then draw the number of sea creatures needed to make the tanks equal.

Activity 37

TEAM SCORES

Fill in the missing number on the scoreboard so the guest team's and home team's scores add up to 8.

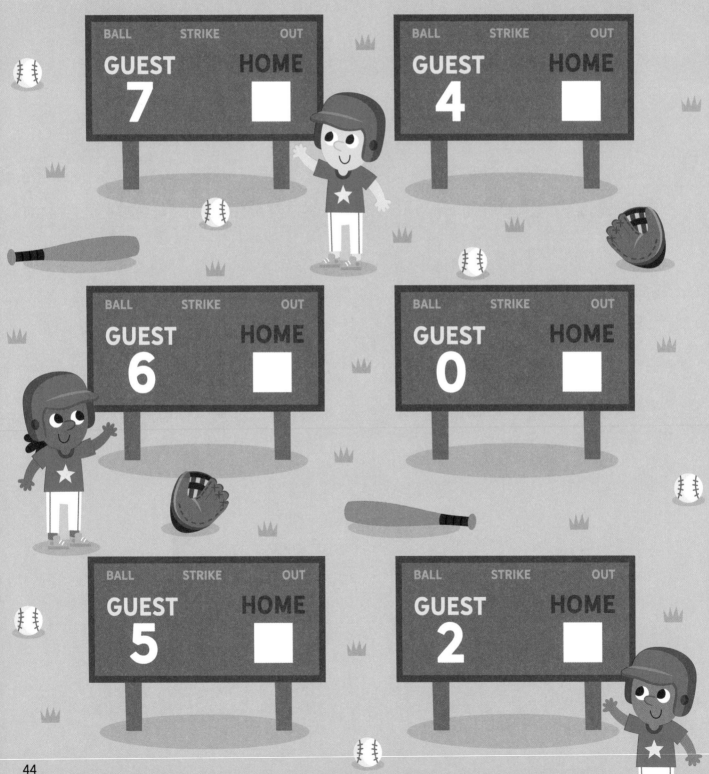

UNLOCK THE CODE

Each set of locks should add up to 9. Fill in the missing number.

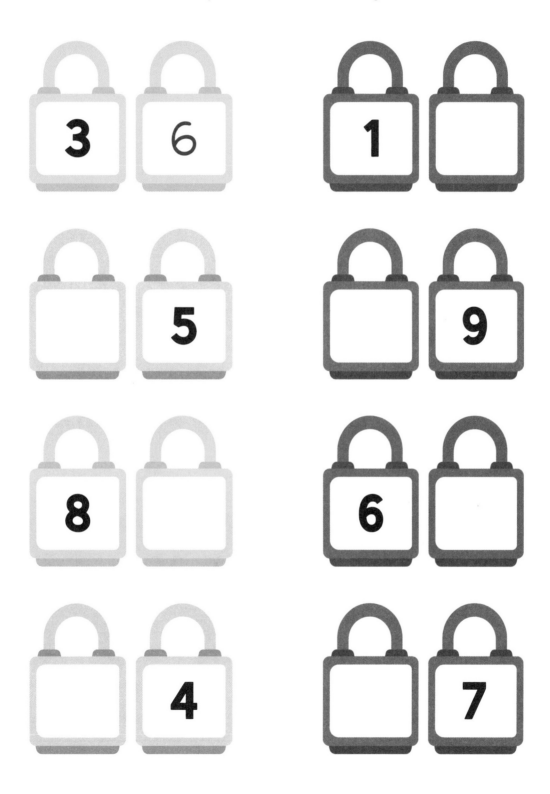

Activity 39

FILL UP THE BOX

Count the objects, then draw the number of objects needed to make the boxes equal.

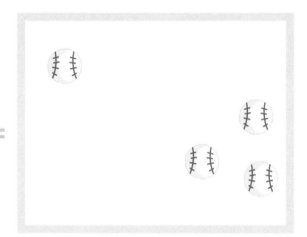

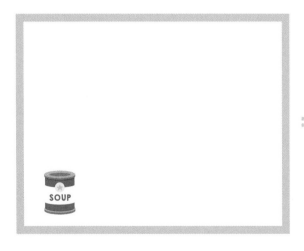

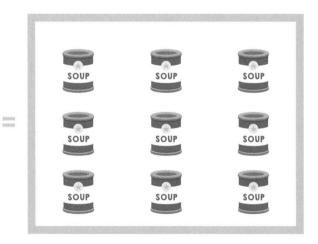

BRACELET BEADS

Draw the number of beads needed so that each bracelet has 10.

Activity 41

PIZZA PARTY

Color the slices of pizza using the instructions below.

Color 2 slices **red** + 4 slices **yellow**

Color 3 slices **red** + 3 slices **yellow**

Color 5 slices **red** + 1 slice **yellow**

Color 4 slices **red** + 2 slices **yellow**

Activity 42

CARD SORT

Which card is missing? Circle the card that completes the set.

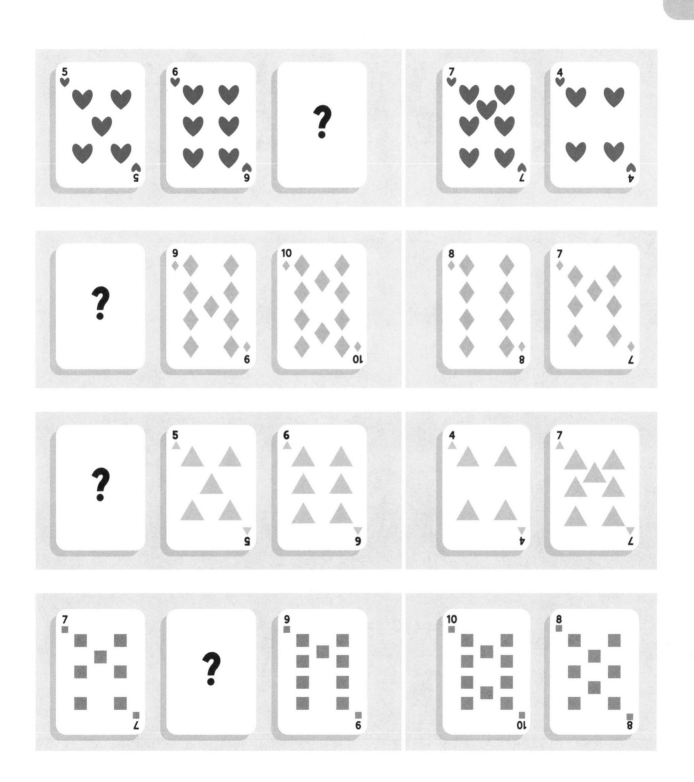

Activity 43

CHOO CHOO LINE

Fill in the missing number so that the train cars are in order. Use the clues to help you.

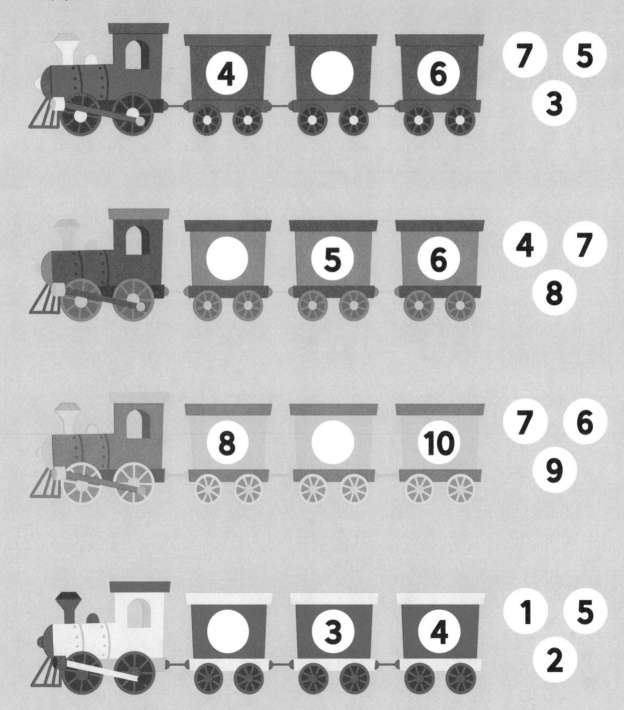

READY, SET, RUN

Which group of runners are NOT in order? Circle the groups.

Activity 45

HALLOWEEN HUNT

Which groups of trick-or-treaters are in a repeating pattern? Circle the groups.

AWESOME ANIMALS

Which animal completes the pattern? Circle the animal.

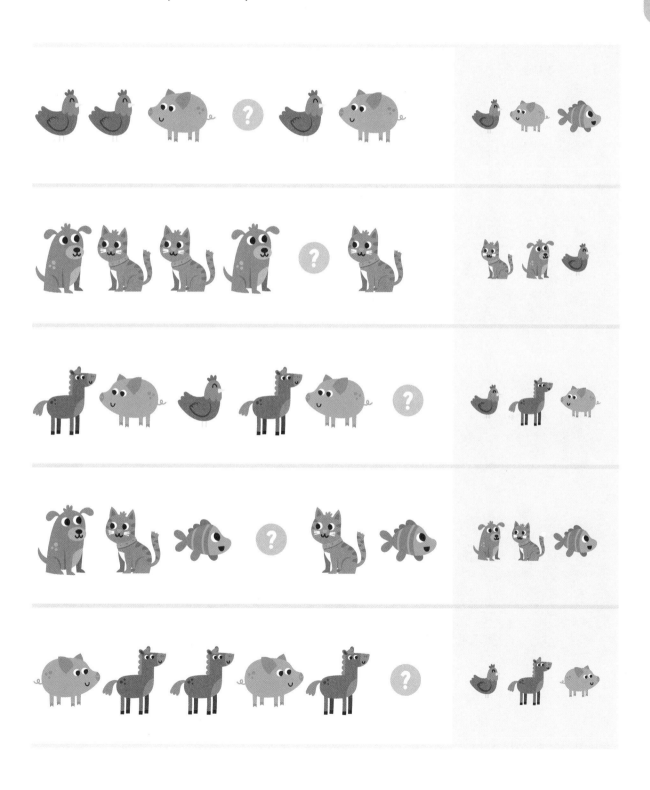

Activity 47

UNLOCK IT

Open the lock by filling in the missing numbers to complete the repeating pattern.

SHAPE MATCH

Circle the item that looks like the shape.

FLAT OR SOLID?

What kind of shape is it? Write F if the shape is FLAT (2-D) or S if it is SOLID (3-D).

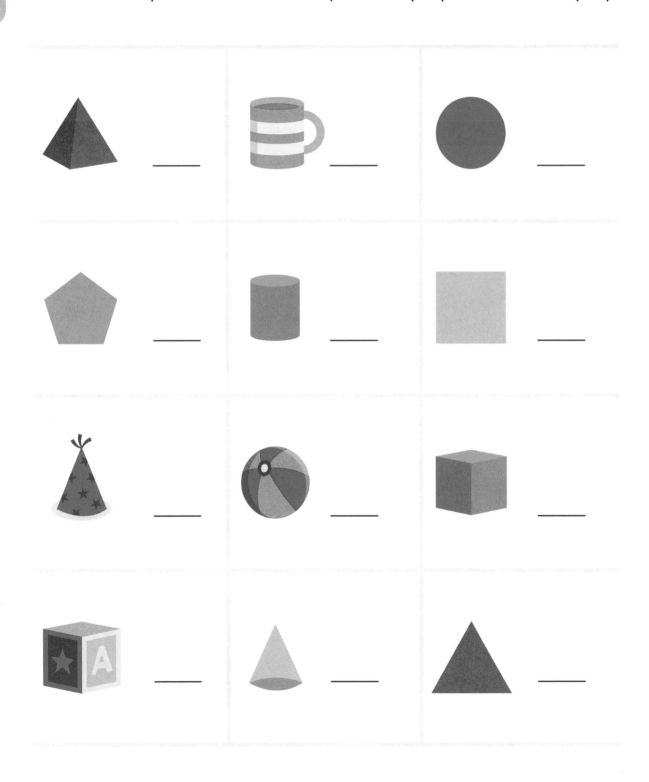

3-D SHAPE FUN

Count the 3-D objects and tally how many you find.

Activity 51

PLAY SPACE

How many rectangular prisms, cubes, and cylinders can you find?
Write the number.

Activity 52

LET'S GO TO THE BEACH

Count the 3-D shapes. How many of each can you find? Write the number.

Activity 53

STACKS OF BOOKS

Put an X on the stack that has the FEWEST books and circle the stack that has the MOST books.

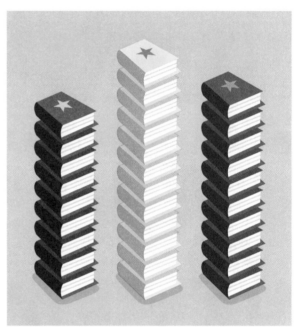

Activity 54

PAIRS OF SHOES

In each pair, circle the SHORTER shoe.

DRAW IT LONGER

Draw the same image but make it LONGER.

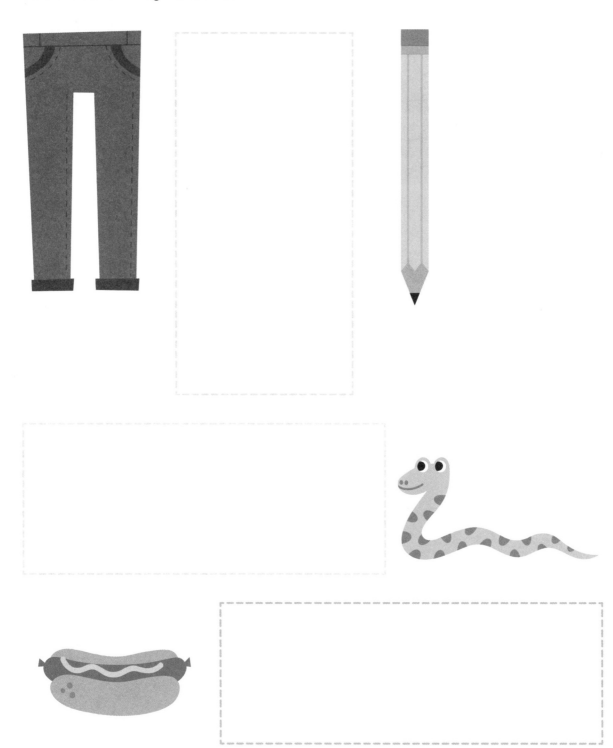

LONGER VS. SHORTER

In each set, write L for the tool that is LONGER and S for the tool that is SHORTER.

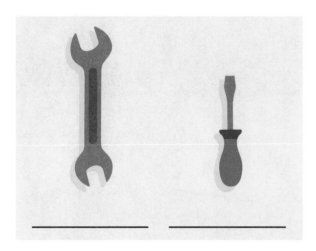

_____   _____

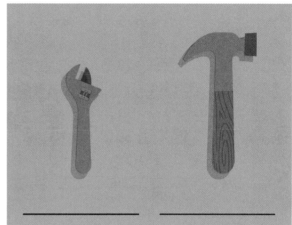

_____   _____

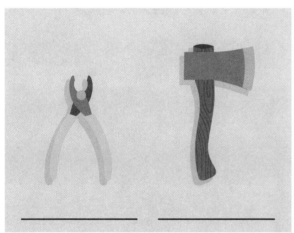

_____   _____

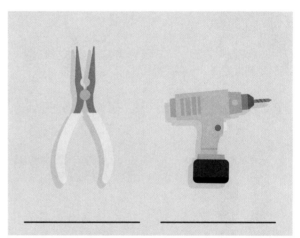

_____   _____

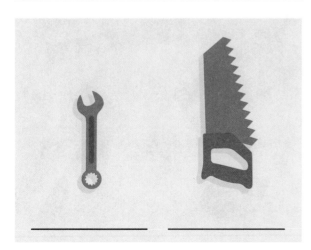

_____   _____

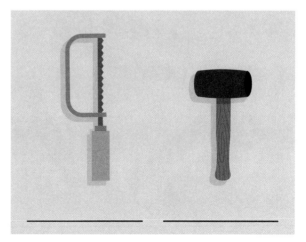

_____   _____

Activity 57

BLUE JEANS

Put an X on all the jeans that are LONGER than the pair on Yusef.

Activity 58
DOGGY TAILS

In each pair, circle the dog with the SHORTER tail.

Activity 59

MORE BOOKS

Compare the groups of books in each set. Circle the group that has MORE books.

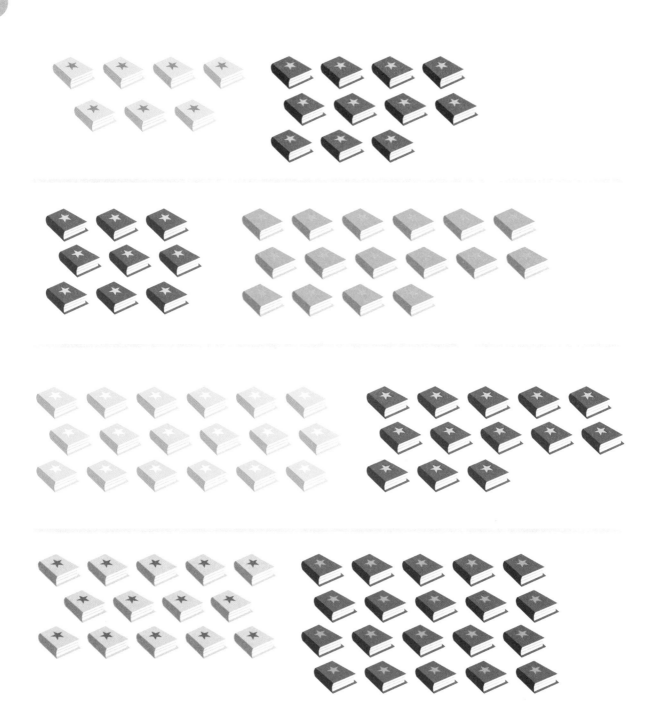

Activity 60

PENNY POWER

Count the pennies in each stack. Draw a line to the matching number.

1 2 3 4 5 6 7 8 9 10 11 12

Activity 61

CANDY STORE

How much does each candy cost? Write the number.

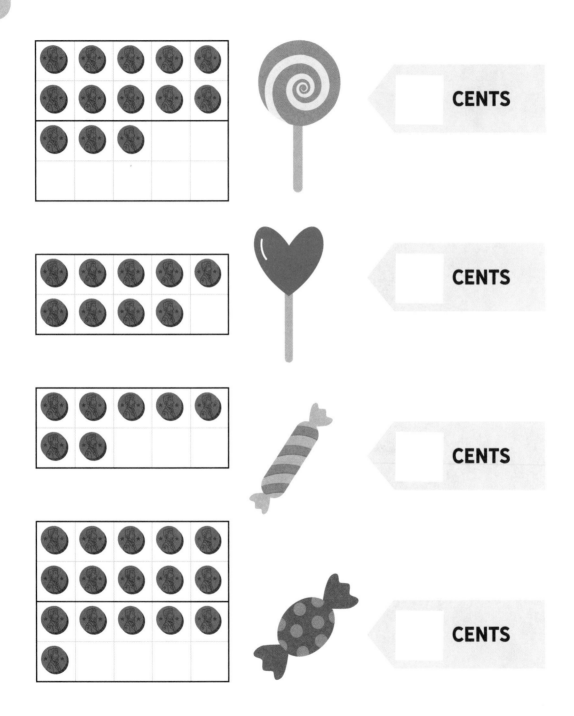

CENTS

CENTS

CENTS

CENTS

FIND 10 PENNIES

Circle the pennies into groups of 10.

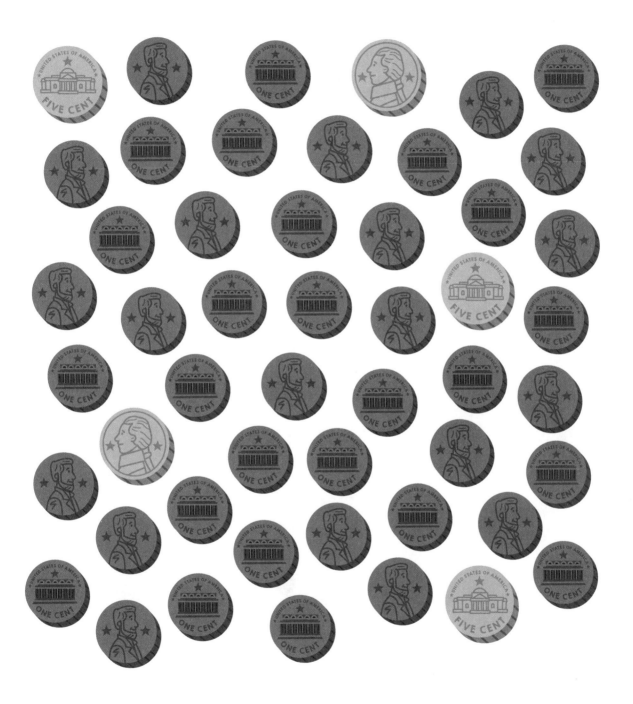

How many groups of 10 did you circle? _____

Activity 63

GROUPING BY 5

Circle groups of 5 pennies. How many groups are there? Write the number.

Number of Groups

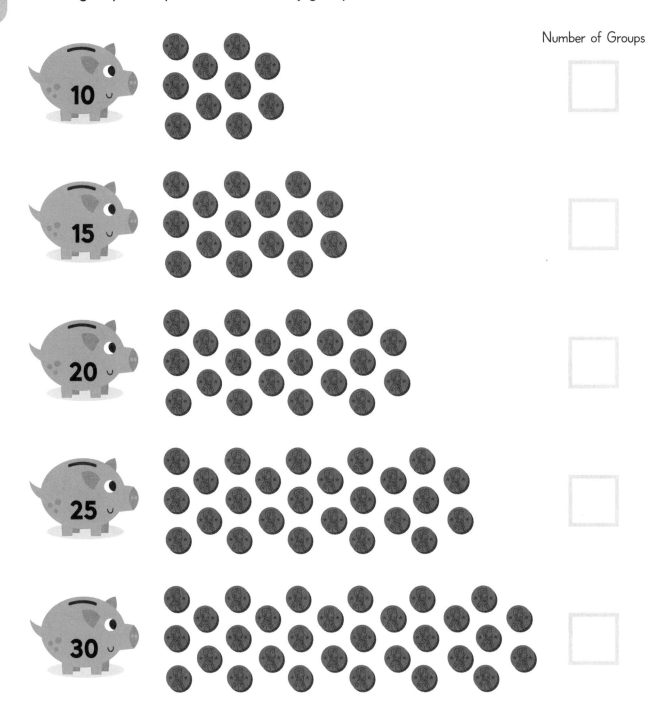

How many groups of 5 do you need to make 50? _____

Activity 64

WHICH HAS MORE?

Put a check mark beneath the stack of dimes that has MORE.

Activity 65

WHICH SIDE IS HEAVIER?

Count the objects on each seesaw and write the number. Circle the side that is HEAVIER.

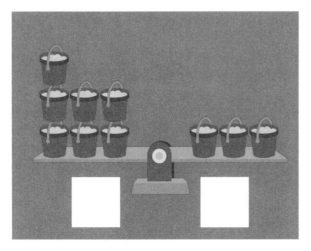

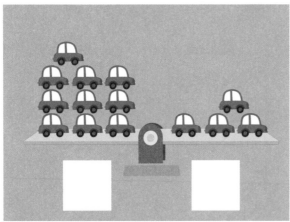

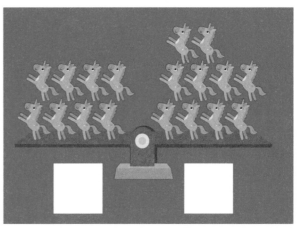

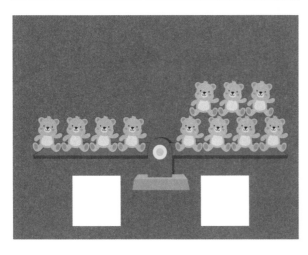

WHICH IS HEAVIER?

Compare the two objects in each set. Circle the object that looks HEAVIER.

Activity 67

WEIGH THE FRUIT

Count the fruit on each scale and write the number. Circle the side that is LIGHTER.

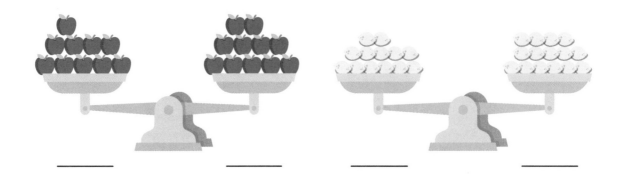

_____   _____   _____   _____

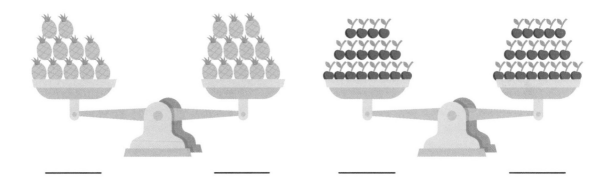

_____   _____   _____   _____

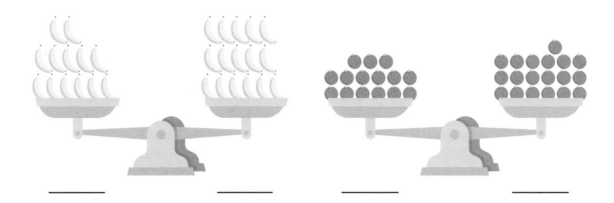

_____   _____   _____   _____

ABOVE VS. BELOW

Color the **cones** ABOVE the line in yellow and color the **cubes** BELOW the line in blue.

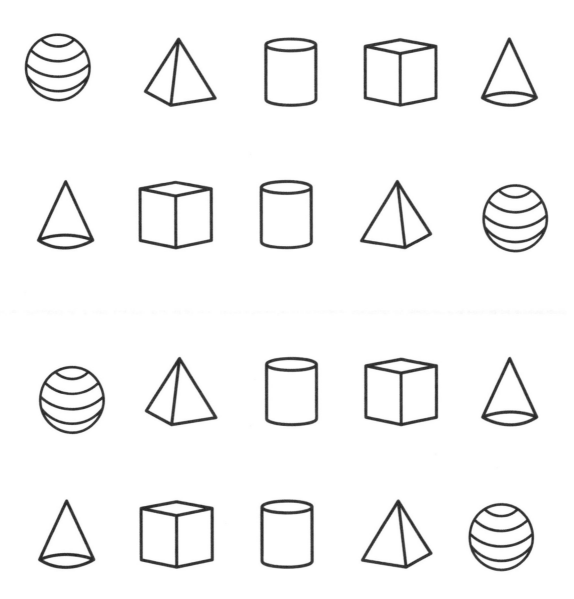

Activity 69

IN FRONT VS. BEHIND

Color the **cylinders** in FRONT of the animals in red, and the **pyramids** BEHIND the animals in green.

Activity 70

COMPARE THE SHAPES

Count the shapes in each set and circle the group that has MORE.

 or

 or

 or

 or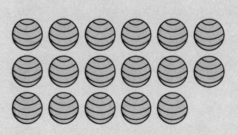

Activity 71

FOLLOW THE TRAIL

Follow the 3-D shapes to get to the end of the trail.

START

FINISH

RUN IN ORDER

Write the missing number on each runner so the numbers are in order.

WRONG RACE CAR

Circle the rows of race cars that are NOT in order.

Activity 74

WHAT'S THE MISSING NUMBER?

Help Naomi finish each set by writing the missing numbers.

1 · 2 · 3 · ☐

4 · 5 · ☐ · 7

14 · 15 · ☐ · ☐

13 · ☐ · 15

3 · ☐ · ☐ · 6

16 · 17 · ☐

HAY DAY

Put an X on the haystacks with numbers that are NOT in order. Connect the Xs to help Hiro the Horse get to the barn.

14 13 16

14 15 16

18 19 20

11 12 13

15 19 16

11 10 19

12 13 14

12 17 13

16 15 19

16 17 18

9 11 10

14 13 15

Activity 76

ODD NUMBERS

Write in the missing odd numbers as you count to 50.

	2		4	
6		8		10
	12		14	
16		18		20
	22		24	
26		28		30
	32		34	
36		38		40
	42		44	
46		48		50

Activity 77

SUMMER FUN

How many seeds are there? Count the seeds in the two watermelon slices and write the number.

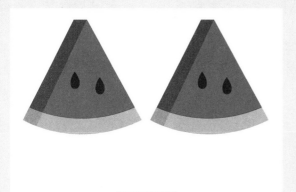

___

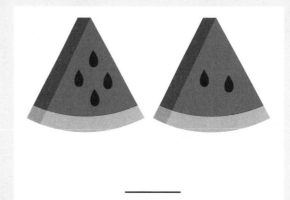

___

___

___

___

___

Activity 78

BUGGY DOWN

Complete each ladybug by drawing dots to make 5 dots in all.

HUNGRY PANDA

How many bamboo stalks are there? Help Pei the Panda count the groups of bamboo and write the number.

Activity 80

MISSING NUMBERS

Write the missing numbers in each row.

1		3	4	5					10
		13			16	17		19	
	22		24			27			
31		33			36			39	
41				45			48		50
	52				56				60
61		63				67			70
	72				76			79	

EVEN NUMBERS

Write in the missing even numbers as you count to 50.

1	3	5
	7	9
11	13	15
	17	19
21	23	25
	27	29
31	33	35
	37	39
41	43	45
	47	49

Activity 82

LADYBUG DOUBLE DOTS

How many dots are on each ladybug? Write the number.

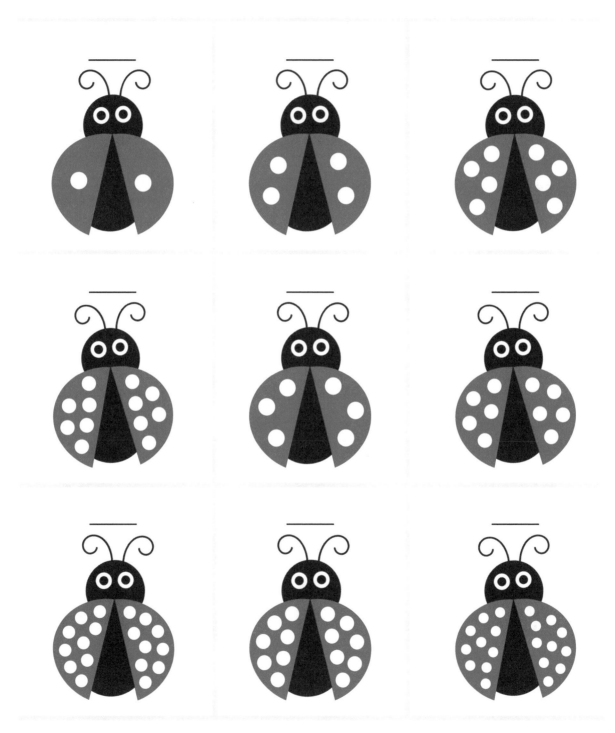

POCKET PENNIES

How many pennies are in each set of pockets? Write the number.

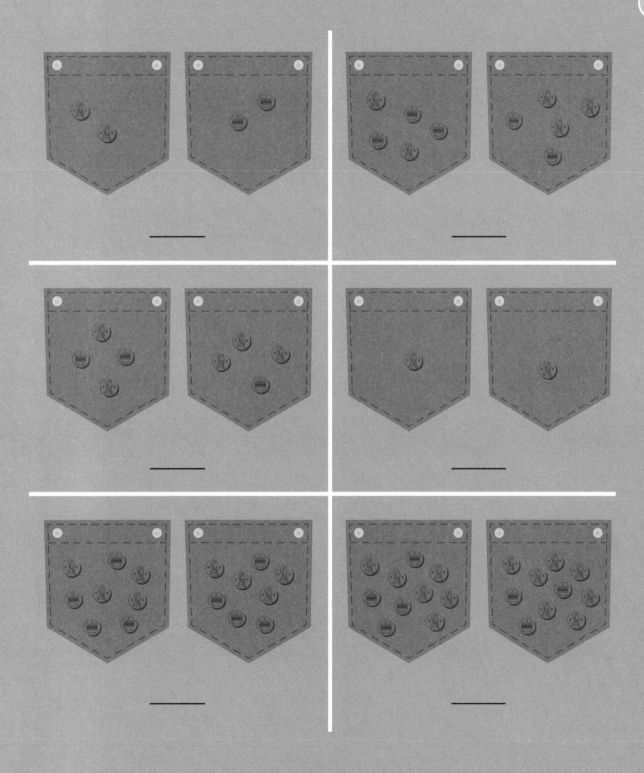

Activity 84

NUMBER THE TOWN

Circle the **even** numbers and put an X on the **odd** numbers. You can look at the charts on Activity 76 and Activity 81 for help.

3

17

16

5 7

8

SHOP

8 2

10

6

Activity 85

A WELCOME SURPRISE

Use the color key to color the number tiles as you count to 100.

8, 18

25, 26, 54, 64, 74

91, 92, 93, 94, 95, 96, 97, 98, 99, 100

56, 57, 66, 67, 76, 77, 86, 87

14, 15, 16, 17, 23, 24, 27, 28, 32, 33, 34, 35, 36, 37, 38, 39

43, 44, 45, 46, 47, 48, 53, 55, 58, 63, 65, 68, 73, 75, 78, 83, 84, 85, 88

1	2	3	4	5	6	7	8	9	10
11	12	13	14	15	16	17	18	19	20
21	22	23	24	25	26	27	28	29	30
31	32	33	34	35	36	37	38	39	40
41	42	43	44	45	46	47	48	49	50
51	52	53	54	55	56	57	58	59	60
61	62	63	64	65	66	67	68	69	70
71	72	73	74	75	76	77	78	79	80
81	82	83	84	85	86	87	88	89	90
91	92	93	94	95	96	97	98	99	100

Activity 86

SHAPE PATTERNS

Fill in the missing shapes to complete the pattern.
Use the color key to color the pattern.

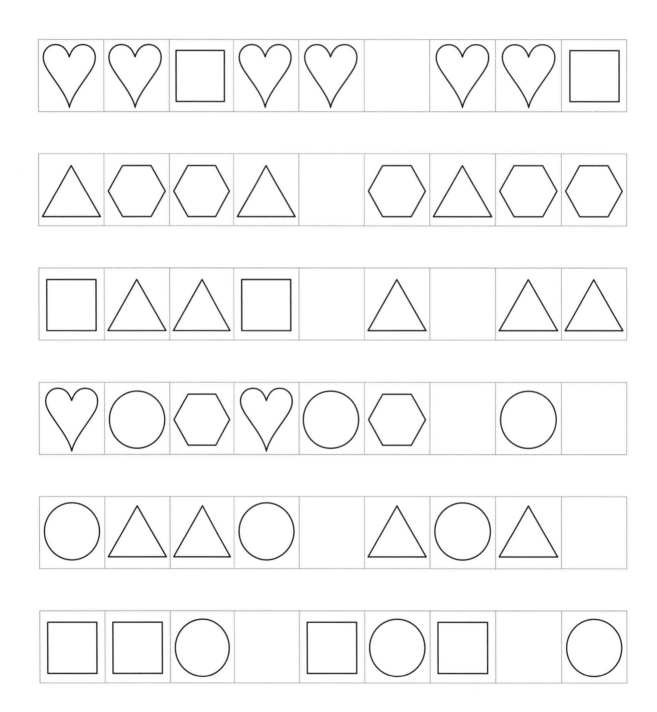

PATTERN POWER

Look at the pattern and circle the number or shape that completes it.

2, 2, 5, 2, 2, 5, 2, 2, ?　　　　　　**2　7　5**

1, 2, 3, 1, 2, 3, 1, ?, 3　　　　　　**1　2　4**

5, 10, 5, 10, ? 10　　　　　　**5　3　10**

10, 20, 30, 10, 20, 30, ?, 20, 30　　　　**10　20　30**

Activity 88

HAPPY HOPPING

Help Fia the Frog jump on lily pads and answer the questions below.

The frog jumps 5 times. What lily pad number does the frog land on? _____

The frog jumps 3 times. What lily pad number does the frog land on? _____

The frog jumps 4 times. What lily pad number does the frog land on? _____

The frog jumps 5 times. What lily pad number does the frog land on? _____

Activity 89

CORNERS AND POINTS

Count the shapes and answer the questions.

How many stars are there? _____

How many points are there
on all the stars together? _____

How many triangles are there? _____

How many points are there
on all the triangles together? _____

How many squares are there? _____

How many corners are there
on all the squares together? _____

How many hexagons are
there? _____

How many points are there
on all the hexagons together? _____

Activity 90

COUNTING BIKES

Use the pictures to help you answer the questions.

How many bikes are there? _____   How many wheels are there? _____

How many bikes are there? _____   How many wheels are there? _____

Activity 91

JUMPING JELLYFISH

Help Juno the Jellyfish jump on the shells and answer the questions below.

The jellyfish jumps 7 times. What shell number does the jellyfish land on? _____

The jellyfish jumps 5 times. What shell number does the jellyfish land on? _____

The jellyfish jumps 6 times. What shell number does the jellyfish land on? _____

The jellyfish jumps 4 times. What shell number does the jellyfish land on? _____

Activity 92

BY THE DOZEN

Using the ten frames, fill in blue and red circles to show different ways to make 12. Answers will vary.

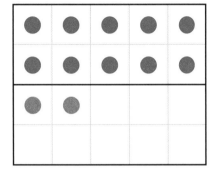

12 = __10__ **+** __2__

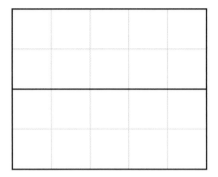

12 = _____ **+** _____

12 = _____ **+** _____

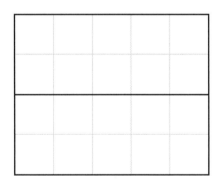

12 = _____ **+** _____

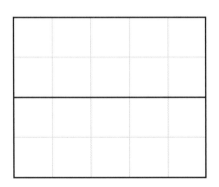

12 = _____ **+** _____

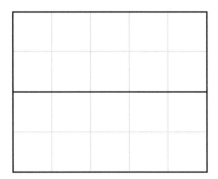

12 = _____ **+** _____

MAKE TWENTY

Using the ten frames, fill in blue and red circles to show different ways to make 20. Answers will vary.

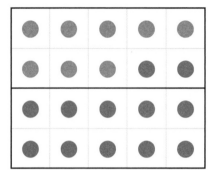

20 = _8_ **+** _12_

20 = ____ **+** ____

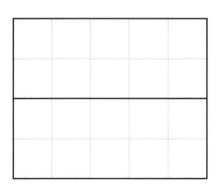

20 = ____ **+** ____

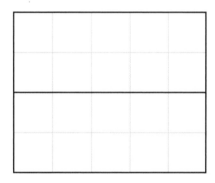

20 = ____ **+** ____

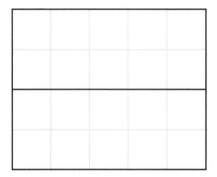

20 = ____ **+** ____

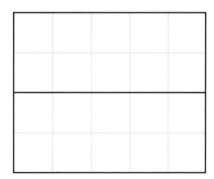

20 = ____ **+** ____

HAPPY HUNDRED

Fill in the missing numbers as you count to 100.

1					
			14	**15**	
		23			
				35	
	42				
51				**55**	
	72				
	82				
			94		

		8		
				20
			29	
46				
			59	
		68		
76	77			
			89	
				100

Activity 95

SEASHELLS BY THE SEASHORE

Circle the groups of seashells to match the number on each bucket.

Activity 96
MORE TREATS

Circle the kid in each pair who has MORE treats.

MAKE FEWER LEAVES

For each green pile, write any number that is LESS than the orange pile. Try not to repeat the answers.

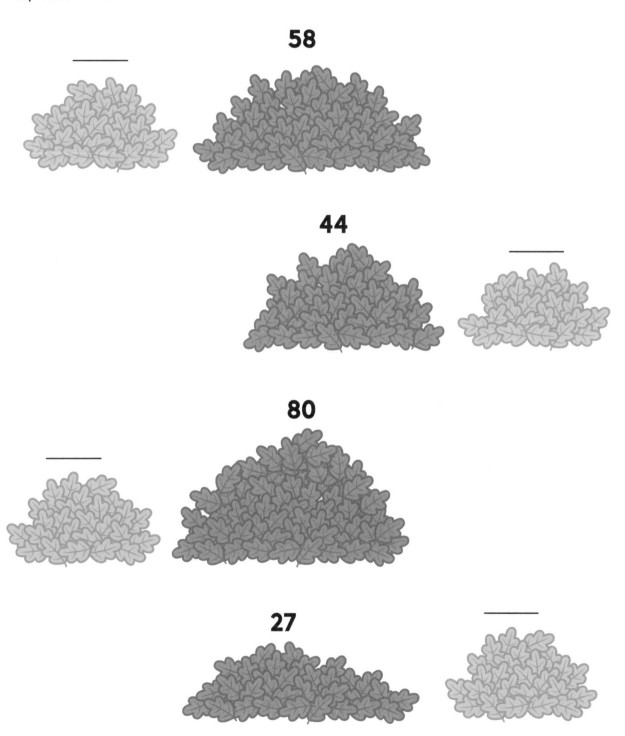

58

44

80

27

Activity 98

GROCERY GRAB

In each pair, circle the grocery bag that has MORE items.

15   42

33   21

24   22

93   71

48   55

76   62

Activity 99

HOW MANY JUMPS?

See where Juno the Jellyfish starts and ends.
Write the number of jumps the jellyfish made.

6

_____

_____

_____

_____

Activity 100

FIND 5s & Os

Find and color every number that ends in 5 or 0.

1	2	3	4	5
11	12	13	14	15
21	22	23	24	25
31	32	33	34	35
41	42	43	44	45
51	52	53	54	55
61	62	63	64	65
71	72	73	74	75
81	82	83	84	85
91	92	93	94	95

6	7	8	9	10
16	17	18	19	20
26	27	28	29	30
36	37	38	39	40
46	47	48	49	50
56	57	58	59	60
66	67	68	69	70
76	77	78	79	80
86	87	88	89	90
96	97	98	99	100

Activity 101

SO MANY MARBLES

Use the marbles to count by 10s and write the numbers to 100.

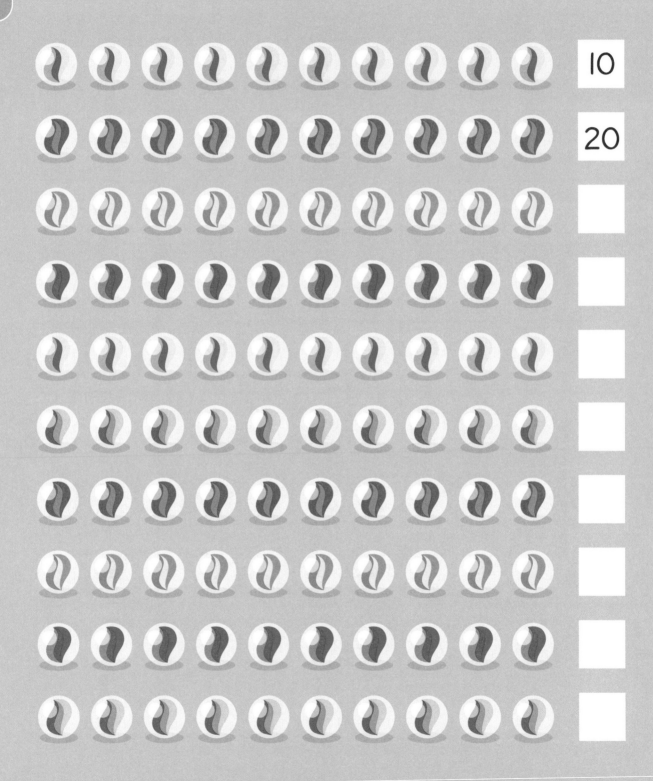

10

20

COUNTING CANS

Use the soda cans to count by 5s and write the numbers to 100.

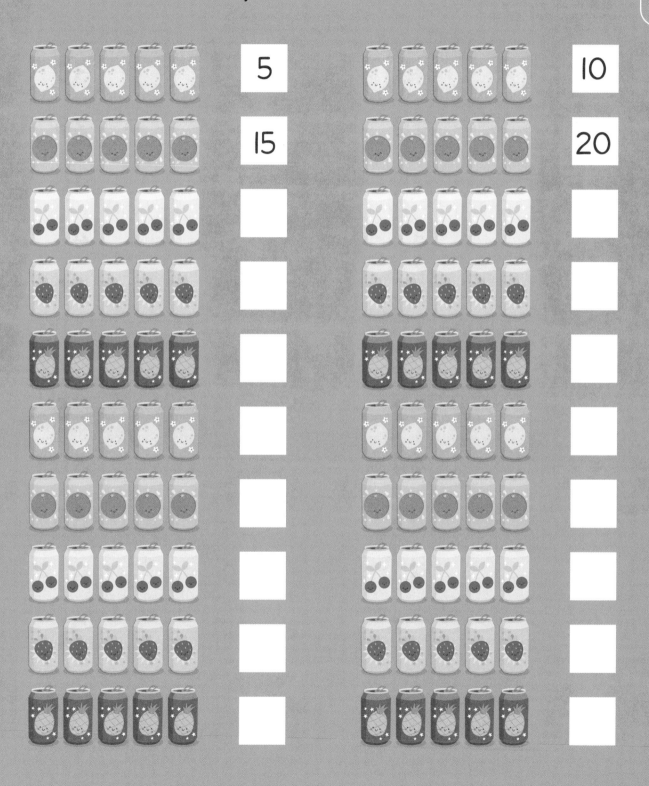

5

10

15

20

Activity 103

COMPLETE THE COUNT

Use the patterns in the chart to write the missing digit in the numbers.

5	15	40	30
10	20	45	35
15	25	50	40
20	3_	55	4_
2<u>5</u>	35	6_	50

12	33	60	75
22	44	70	80
32	55	_0	85
4_	6_	90	9_
5_	_7	__0	9_

MAKE THE NUMBER

Put an X on the extra nickels so you are left with the number on the piggy bank.

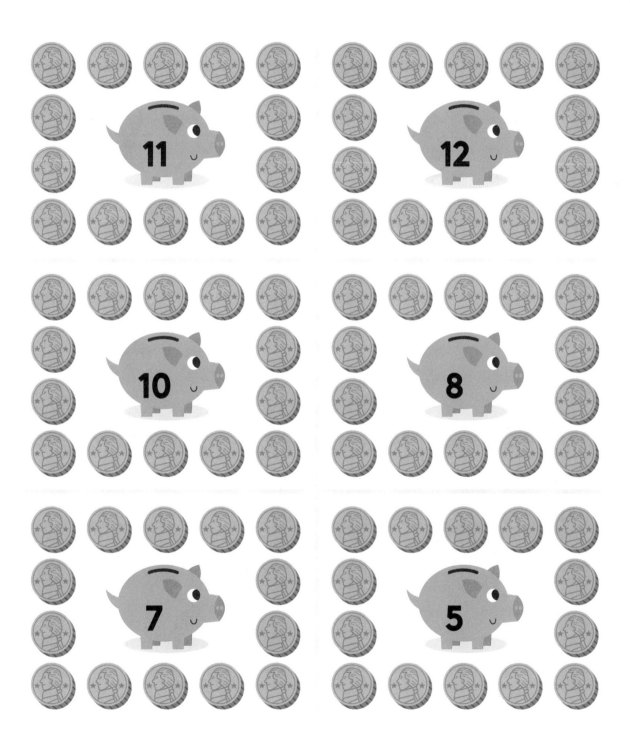

Activity 105

LET'S MAKE SOME CENTS

Draw the number of pennies needed to buy each toy.

WHAT'S THE EQUATION?

Draw a line from the equation to the matching number line.

3 + 2 = 5

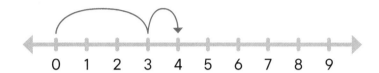

3 + 1 = 4

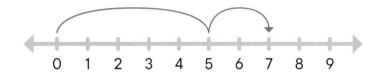

5 + 2 = 7

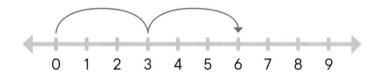

6 + 2 = 8

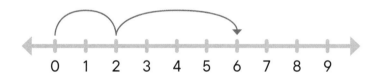

2 + 4 = 6

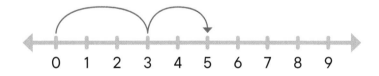

3 + 3 = 6

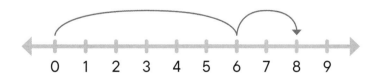

Activity 107

FREEZE TAG

Draw a picture for each problem to help you solve it and write the answer.
Explain to an adult how you got your answer.

10 kids are playing freeze tag. 4 are frozen.
How many are still moving? _____

12 kids are playing freeze tag. 8 are frozen.
How many are still moving? _____

14 kids are playing freeze tag. 7 are frozen.
How many are still moving? _____

Activity 108

HOW MANY HOPS?

See where Fia the Frog starts and ends.
Write the number of hops the frog made.

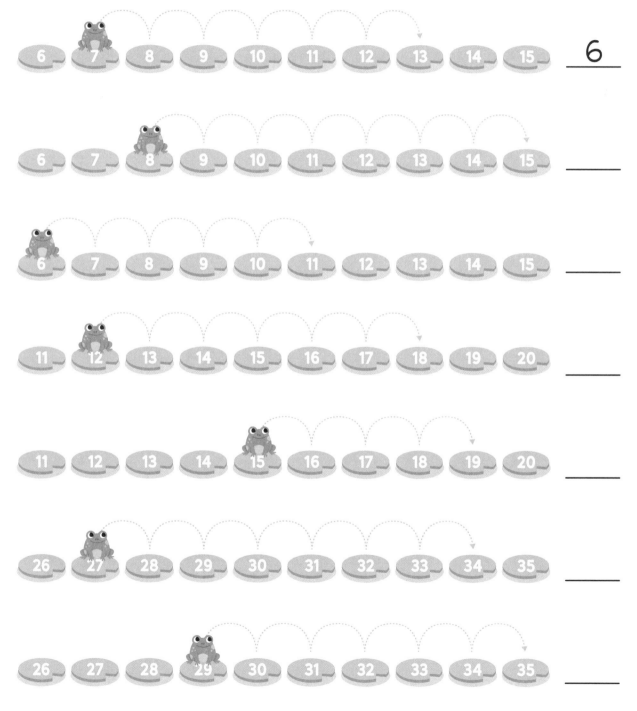

6

Activity 109

PENNY PROBLEMS

Draw a picture for each problem to help you solve it and write the answer.
Explain to an adult how you got your answer.

Eli has 9 pennies. He got more pennies from Ava.
Now he has 14 pennies. How many pennies did Ava give him? _____

Ava has 20 pennies. She gave some to Eli.
Now she has 15 pennies. How many did she give to Eli? _____

JUMP! JUMP!

Count how many jumps the athlete needs to get to the number where the star is.

3 4 5 6 7 8 9 ____

4 5 6 7 8 9 10 ____

5 6 7 8 9 10 11 ____

6 7 8 9 10 11 12 ____

7 8 9 10 11 12 13 ____

Activity 111

TAKE THE TACOS

Elliot ate 2 tacos on each plate. On each taco plate, put an X on 2 tacos, then write the remaining amount.

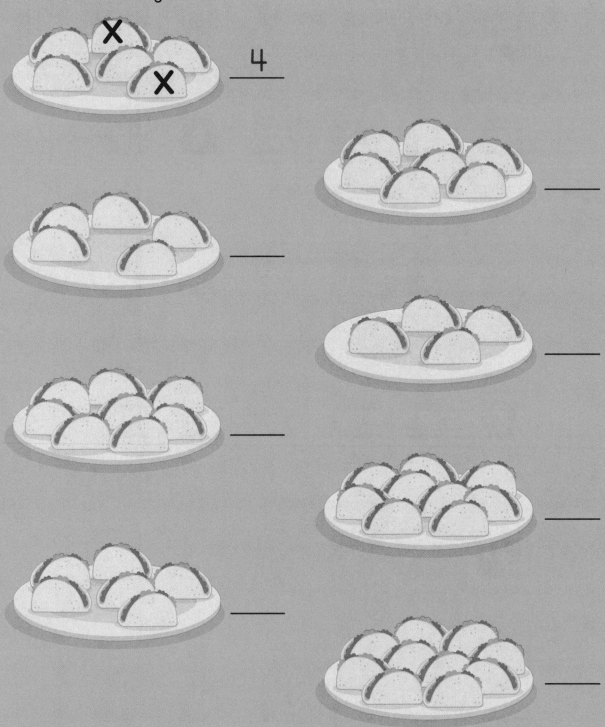

Activity 112

AQUATIC LIFE

In each group, put an X on 4 sea creatures, then complete the subtraction equation.

$$8 - 4 = 4$$

$$\boxed{} - 4 = \boxed{}$$

$$\boxed{} - 4 = \boxed{}$$

$$\boxed{} - 4 = \boxed{}$$

$$\boxed{} - 4 = \boxed{}$$

Activity 113

OUT OF THE PARK

Cross out the number of balls called by the umpire, then complete the subtraction equation.

4 − 2 = 2

□ − □ = □

□ − □ = □

□ − □ = □

□ − □ = □

□ − □ = □

Activity 114

SHOPPING FUN

Lucas bought some items. Cross out the number of dollars he used for each item and complete the subtraction equation.

$$9 \; - \; 4 \; = \; 5$$

$$\underline{\quad} \; - \; 8 \; = \; \underline{\quad}$$

$$\underline{\quad} \; - \; 6 \; = \; \underline{\quad}$$

$$\underline{\quad} \; - \; 7 \; = \; \underline{\quad}$$

JORDAN'S RAMEN

Draw a picture for each problem to help you solve it and
write the answer. Explain to an adult how you got your answer.

Jordan has 12 ramen packs.
In a week he ate 8 of them. How many packs are left?   _____

Jordan makes 3 bowls of ramen on Saturday, 2 bowls on Sunday,
and 4 bowls on Monday. How many bowls of ramen did he make?   _____

Activity 116
FALLING PETALS

Count the number of petals remaining on the flower, then complete the subtraction equation.

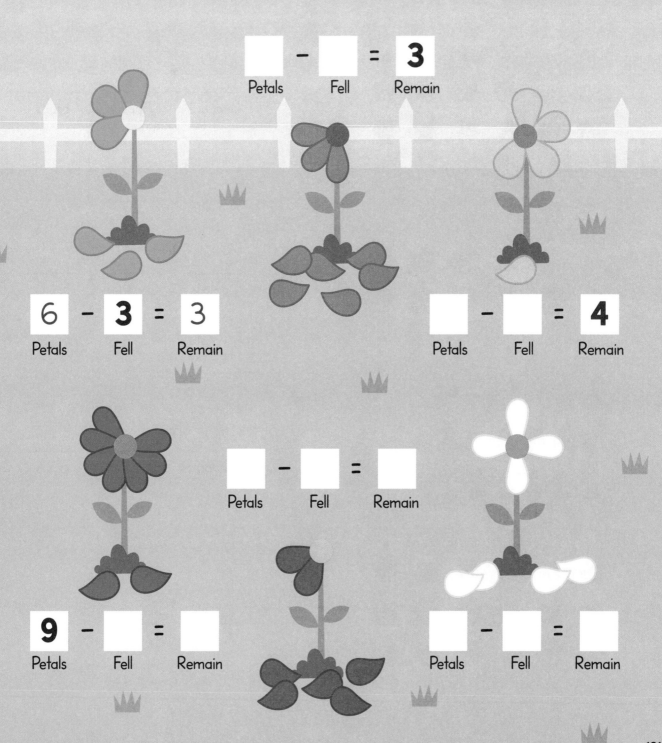

☐ − ☐ = **3**
Petals　　Fell　　Remain

6 − **3** = 3
Petals　　Fell　　Remain

☐ − ☐ = **4**
Petals　　Fell　　Remain

☐ − ☐ = ☐
Petals　　Fell　　Remain

9 − ☐ = ☐
Petals　　Fell　　Remain

☐ − ☐ = ☐
Petals　　Fell　　Remain

131

Activity 117

FRUIT BASKET

Count the fruit in each group and make an addition equation.

_____ + _____ = _____
Bananas   Apples   Fruits

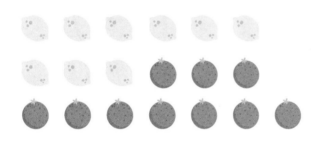

_____ + _____ = _____
Lemons   Oranges   Fruits

_____ + _____ = _____
Pineapples   Cherries   Fruits

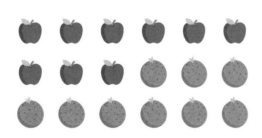

_____ + _____ = _____
Apples   Oranges   Fruits

Activity 118

CANDY COUNT

Circle the candy box that correctly matches the addition equation.

Which box shows 5 + 6 = 11?

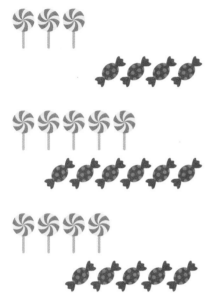

Which box shows 6 + 6 = 12?

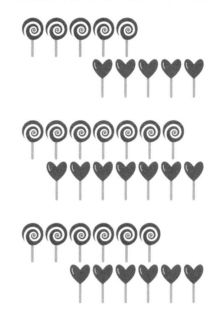

Which box shows 7 + 3 = 10?

Which box shows 2 + 8 = 10?

Activity 119

FISH FRIENDS

Count the fish in each group and add them together to solve the addition equation.

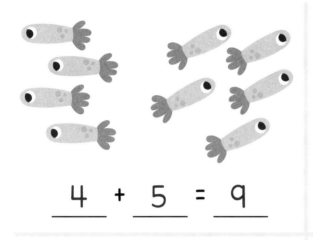

$$\underline{\ \ 4\ \ } + \underline{\ \ 5\ \ } = \underline{\ \ 9\ \ }$$

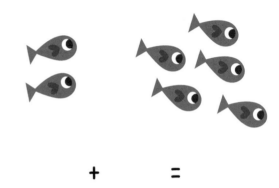

$$\underline{\hspace{1cm}} + \underline{\hspace{1cm}} = \underline{\hspace{1cm}}$$

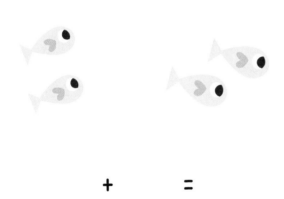

$$\underline{\hspace{1cm}} + \underline{\hspace{1cm}} = \underline{\hspace{1cm}}$$

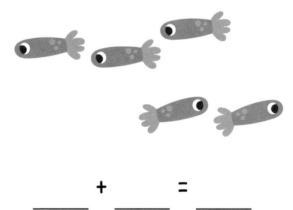

$$\underline{\hspace{1cm}} + \underline{\hspace{1cm}} = \underline{\hspace{1cm}}$$

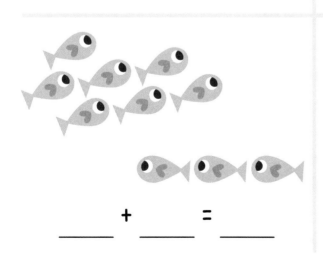

$$\underline{\hspace{1cm}} + \underline{\hspace{1cm}} = \underline{\hspace{1cm}}$$

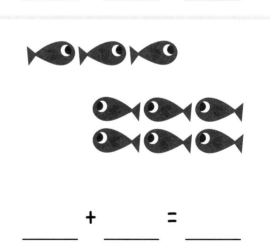

$$\underline{\hspace{1cm}} + \underline{\hspace{1cm}} = \underline{\hspace{1cm}}$$

BRUNO'S BIKE RIDES

Draw a picture for each problem to help you solve it and write the answer. Explain to an adult how you got your answer.

Bruno rode his bike 3 times on Saturday. Then he rode his bike 6 times on Sunday. How many times did he ride? _____

Bruno rode his bike with 5 friends yesterday. Today he rode with 7 new friends. How many friends did he ride with all together? _____

Activity 121

ADD ME UP

Complete the addition equations using the number lines.

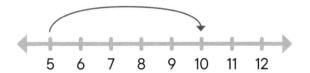

5 + _____ = _____

4 + _____ = _____

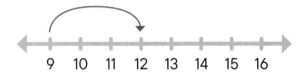

9 + _____ = _____

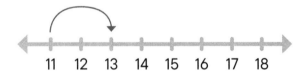

11 + _____ = _____

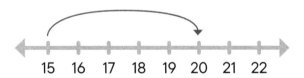

15 + _____ = _____

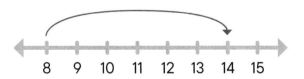

8 + _____ = _____

Activity 122

CLASS ACT

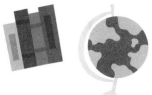

Draw a picture for each problem to help you solve it and write the answer. Explain to an adult how you got your answer.

A classroom has 8 students.
6 students go outside to recess. How many students are left?   _____

There are 7 students in the classroom.
8 more students come inside.
Now how many students are in the classroom?   _____

Activity 123

BIRDBATH

For each fountain, choose two groups of birds, then make an addition equation. Answers will vary.

4	+	2	=	6

$$\boxed{} + \boxed{} = \boxed{}$$

$$\boxed{} + \boxed{} = \boxed{}$$

$$\boxed{} + \boxed{} = \boxed{}$$

$$\boxed{} + \boxed{} = \boxed{}$$

$$\boxed{} + \boxed{} = \boxed{}$$

Activity 124

PICKING FRUIT

For each cart, pick two groups of fruit, then draw them to make an addition equation. Answers will vary.

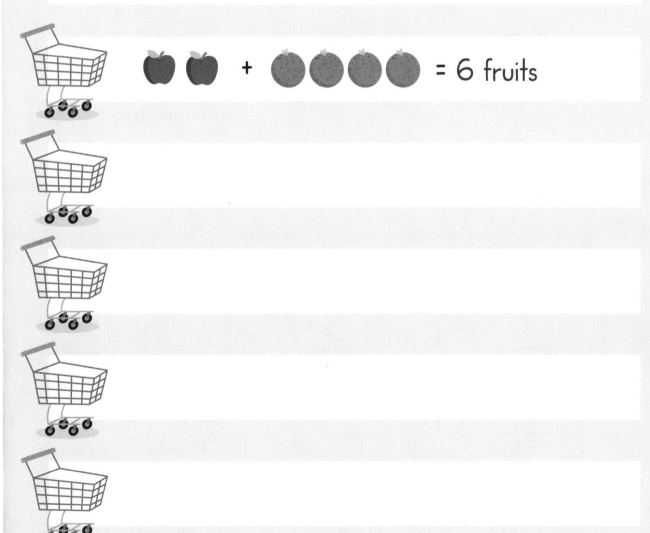

MAKE YOUR OWN BREAKFAST

How many eggs and waffles do you want on your plate? Select from the numbers below each item. Make 5 plates. Answers will vary.

$$\underline{6} \quad + \quad \underline{2} \quad = \quad \underline{8}$$

Waffles   Eggs   Total food

| 5, 6, 4, 7, 3 | 10, 2, 12, 1, 8 | How many items are on the plate? |

_____ + _____ = _____
Waffles   Eggs   Total food

_____ + _____ = _____
Waffles   Eggs   Total food

_____ + _____ = _____
Waffles   Eggs   Total food

_____ + _____ = _____
Waffles   Eggs   Total food

_____ + _____ = _____
Waffles   Eggs   Total food

LEVEL 3

FLY SWAT

Cross out the number of flies shown on the swatter. Write in the remaining amount to complete the subtraction equation.

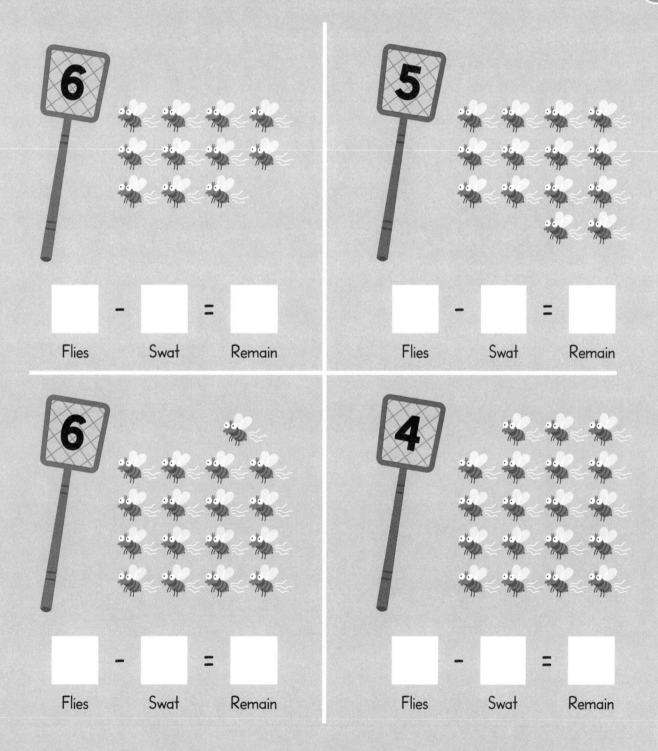

	-		=	
Flies		Swat		Remain

	-		=	
Flies		Swat		Remain

	-		=	
Flies		Swat		Remain

	-		=	
Flies		Swat		Remain

Activity 127

BROKEN WINDOWS

Count the windowpanes, then subtract the broken ones to complete the subtraction equation.

6 − 2 = 4

☐ − ☐ = ☐

☐ − ☐ = ☐

☐ − ☐ = ☐

Activity 128

SHAKE THE TREE

Count the number of leaves on the tree and on the ground, then complete the subtraction equation.

$$\underline{17} - \underline{6} = \underline{11}$$
Leaves   Fell   Remain

$$\underline{} - \underline{} = \underline{}$$
Leaves   Fell   Remain

$$\underline{} - \underline{} = \underline{}$$
Leaves   Fell   Remain

$$\underline{} - \underline{} = \underline{}$$
Leaves   Fell   Remain

Activity 129

LITTLE BIRDS

Read the problem and then count the birds to figure out how many are hiding.
Write the answer.

10 birds are playing hide-and-seek.
How many are hiding in the bush? _____

10 birds are playing hide-and-seek.
How many are hiding in the bush? _____

12 birds are playing hide-and-seek.
How many are hiding in the bush? _____

12 birds are playing hide-and-seek.
How many are hiding in the bush? _____

KYLE'S POINTS

Draw a picture for each problem to help you solve it and write the answer.
Explain to an adult how you got your answer.

Kyle scored 10 points in the first half of the basketball game.
Then he scored more points in the second half.
When it was over, he had 18 points.
How many points did he score in the second half? _____

On Saturday Kyle scored 8 points.
He scored some points on Sunday.
After the two games, he had 20 points.
How many points did he score on Sunday? _____

Activity 131

HOW MANY BIRDS?

Draw a picture for each problem to help you solve it and
write the answer. Explain to an adult how you got your answer.

There are some birds in a tree. 5 more birds land on the tree.
Now there are 13 birds. How many birds were there in the beginning?   _____

13 birds in a birdbath got scared when a car honked a horn.
4 birds flew away. How many birds are left in the tree?   _____

There are 9 birds in a tree. 11 more birds join.
How many birds are there now?   _____

Activity 132

PIZZA PARTY

Count all the slices of pizza on each pan. Put an X on the slices that are eaten and make a subtraction equation. Answers will vary.

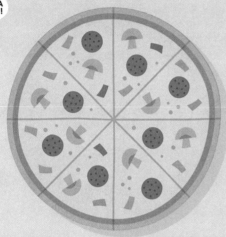

8 – ____ = ____   **6** – ____ = ____

____ – ____ = ____   ____ – ____ = ____

Activity 133

HIT THE TARGET

How many carnival toys and treats are there? Write the number.

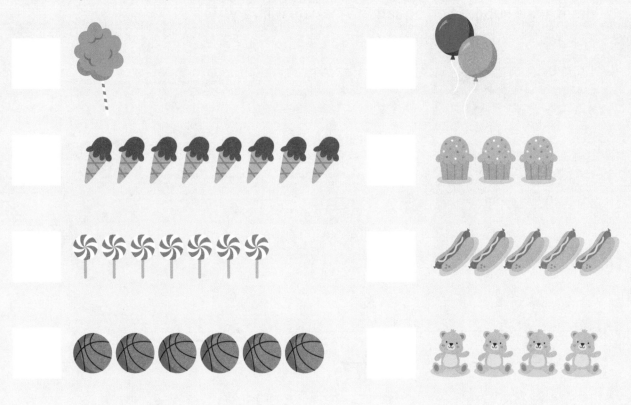

Using the numbers above, fill in the boxes with numbers that add up to the target number. Answers will vary.

Activity 134

WHAT DO YOU NOTICE?

Describe to an adult what you see in the box of donuts below. Use numbers and descriptions.

Activity 135

COLOR THE EGGS

Color in the rest of the carton a different color, to make it full, then complete the addition equation.

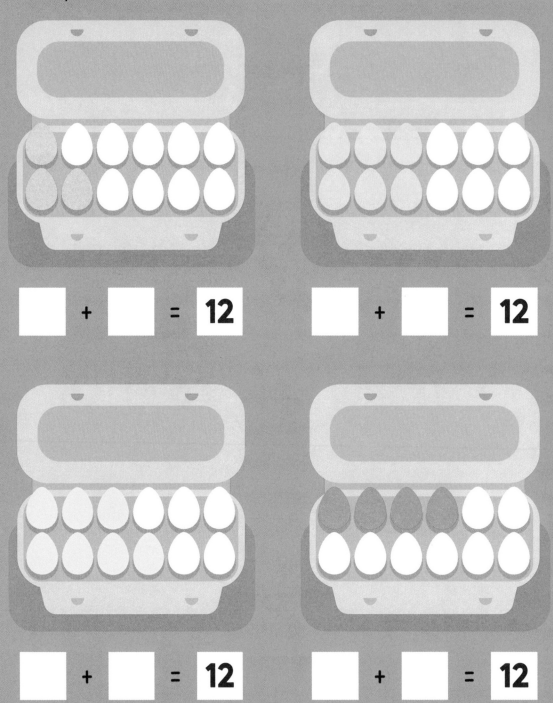

| | + | | = | **12** |

| | + | | = | **12** |

| | + | | = | **12** |

| | + | | = | **12** |

SHOT SUBTRACTION

Count the number of basketballs with Xs on them, then complete the subtraction equation.

$$\underline{\quad 7 \quad} - \underline{\quad 3 \quad} = \underline{\quad 4 \quad}$$

$$\underline{\qquad} - \underline{\qquad} = \underline{\qquad}$$

$$\underline{\qquad} - \underline{\qquad} = \underline{\qquad}$$

$$\underline{\qquad} - \underline{\qquad} = \underline{\qquad}$$

Activity 137

FUN AT THE PARK

Follow the maze and choose the right answer to each subtraction equation to continue.

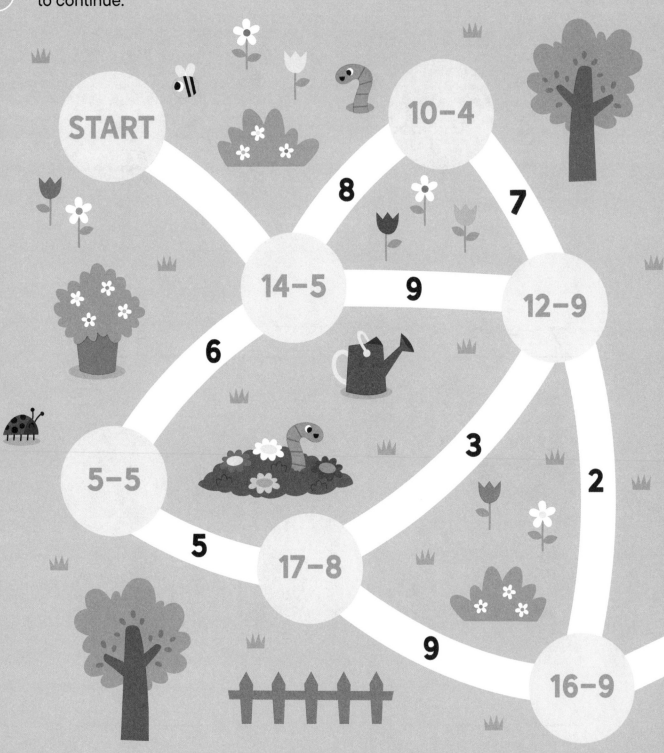

START

10−4

8   7

14−5   9   12−9

6

5−5   3

2

5   17−8

9

16−9

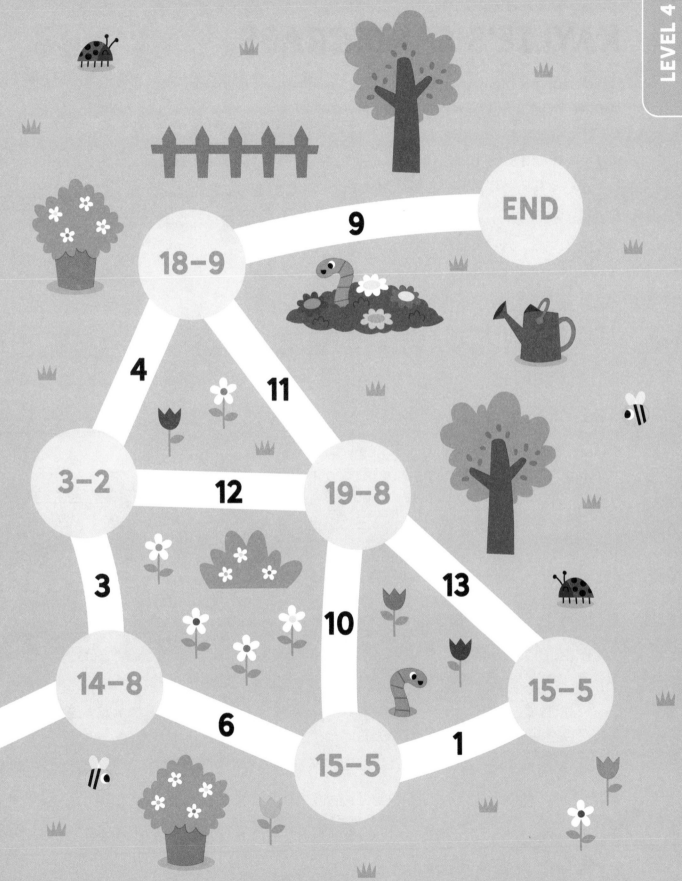

Activity 138

KAYLIE'S SAND CRABS

Read each problem, then draw to solve and write the answer.
Explain to an adult how you got your answer.

Kaylie found 6 sand crabs on the beach. Willie found 14 sand crabs.
How many did they find all together? _____

Kaylie put 20 sand crabs in a bucket. 8 crawled out.
How many sand crabs are still in the bucket? _____

Kaylie took 9 sand crabs and put them in 3 buckets
so each bucket had the same number of sand crabs.
How many sand crabs are in each bucket? _____

TRUE OR FALSE?

Write T if the sentence is true. Write F if it is false.

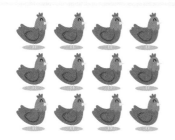 is more than 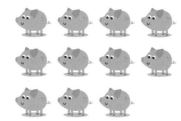 _____

 is less than  _____

 is more than  _____

5 is the same as 3 + 2. _____

12 is the same as 7 + 5. _____

Activity 140

BACKYARD BBQ

Count the food and solve the addition equation.

_____ + _____ = _____

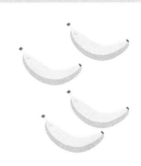  

_____ + _____ = _____

_____ + _____ = _____

_____ + _____ = _____

YUMMY FRIES

Draw a picture for each problem to help you solve it and write the answer. Explain to an adult how you got your answer.

If you eat 5 french fries and then eat 4 more fries, how many fries did you eat?   _____

Four people all get 2 packs of french fries. How many packs of fries did they get all together?   _____

Activity 142

SPACE SUBTRACTION

Circle the correct subtraction equation that matches the spaceship shooting asteroids. Write in the answer.

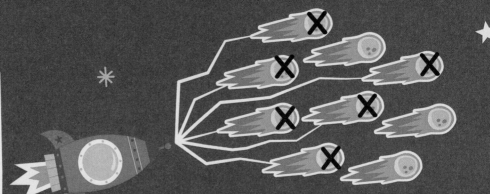

5 – 5 =

9 – 6 =

14 – 9 =

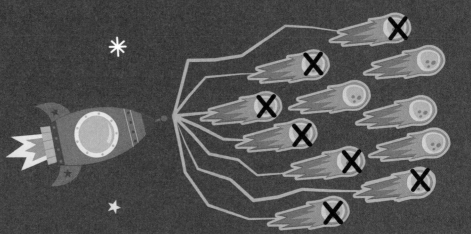

10 – 6 =

13 – 5 =

11 – 7 =

7 – 5 =

12 – 5 =

13 – 4 =

14 – 9 =

15 – 8 =

9 – 5 =

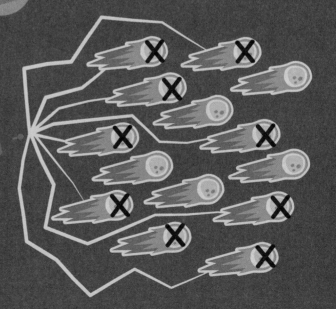

159

Activity 143

BYE-BYE, BIRDIES

Count the birds in each tree. Put an X to cross out how many fly away, then make a subtraction equation. Answers will vary.

_____ − _____ = _____   _____ − _____ = _____

_____ − _____ = _____   _____ − _____ = _____

SHAPES AWAY

Draw the shapes and add Xs to show the subtraction equation.

Draw 12 – 4 = 8 using squares.

Draw 14 – 3 = 11 using circles.

Draw 15 – 8 = 7 using triangles.

Draw 13 – 6 = 7 using rectangles.

Draw 10 – 1 = 9 using hexagons.

Activity 145

HOW MANY ARE HIDING?

Draw a picture for each problem to help you solve it and write the answer. Explain to an adult how you got your answer.

20 birds are playing hide-and-seek. You can see 12 birds.
How many are hiding?   _____

18 birds are playing hide-and-seek. 6 birds fly to the tree.
How many are hiding?   _____

15 birds are playing hide-and-seek. You can see 4 birds.
How many are hiding?   _____

FALLING LEAVES

Circle the correct equation for each tree. Fill in the answer to the subtraction equation.

8 – 5 = ___

9 – 5 = ___

12 – 4 = ___

10 – 6 = ___

10 – 7 = ___

9 – 7 = ___

11 – 6 = ___

11 – 8 = ___

11 – 5 = ___

Activity 147

JENNIFER'S COOKIES

Draw a picture for each problem to help you solve it and
write the answer. Explain to an adult how you got your answer.

Jennifer made some cookies for a party. Dailyn ate 4 cookies, leaving
15 cookies on the plate. How many cookies did Jennifer make?   _____

Jennifer made some cookies for school. She gave the teacher 6 cookies
and has 11 cookies left for her friends. How many cookies did she make?   _____

Jennifer made 8 cookies for Jordan, Kyle, Dailyn, and Aly.
How many cookies can each friend get if they get the same amount?   _____

DONUT DAY

Draw a picture for each problem to help you solve it and write the answer. Explain to an adult how you got your answer.

4 people want to share 8 donuts so they all get the same amount. How many donuts does each person get? _____

The same 4 people want to share 16 donuts so they all get the same amount. How many donuts does each person get? _____

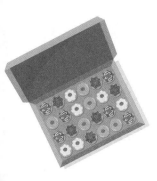

Activity 149

COMPLETE THE CLOCK

Write in the missing numbers to complete each clock.

Activity 150

WHAT TIME IS IT?

Complete the numbers on the clock and draw a line to the correct activity for that time.

AM

PM

PM

PM

Activity 151

AROUND THE CLOCK

Fill in the missing numbers by counting each minute on the clock.

READING MINUTES BY 5s

Fill in the missing numbers by counting every 5 minutes on the clock.

MY TEAMMATES

Create two teams to match the totals. Each team doesn't have to have the same number of players. Answers will vary.

10 PLAYERS

TEAM 1

TEAM 2

12 PLAYERS

TEAM 1

TEAM 2

14 PLAYERS

TEAM 1

TEAM 2

16 PLAYERS

TEAM 1

TEAM 2

Activity 154

TOOLBOX

Draw a line to split the tools into two groups, then write an addition equation to match. Answers will vary.

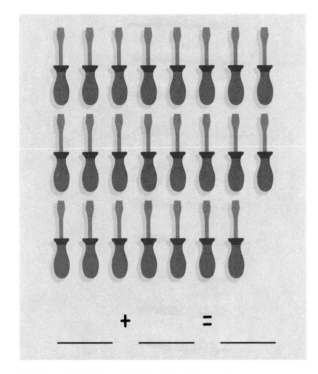

\+ _____ = _____ _____

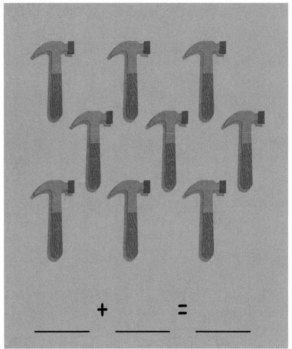

\+ _____ = _____ _____

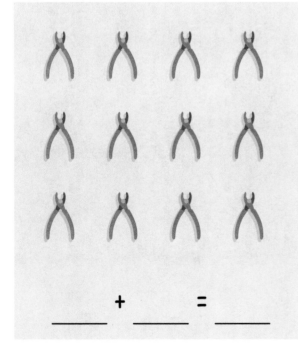

\+ _____ = _____ _____

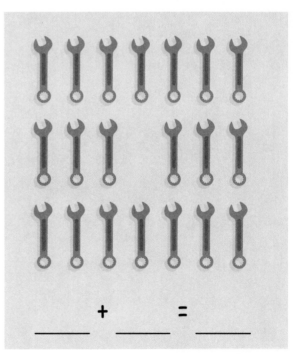

\+ _____ = _____ _____

Activity 155

GONE FISHING

Circle a group of fish to take home, then write a subtraction equation to match.
Answers will vary.

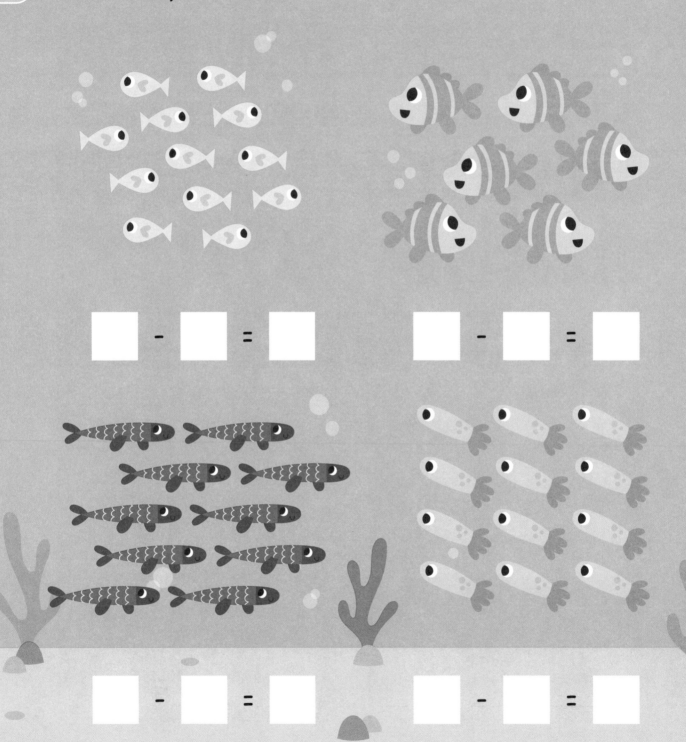

Activity 156
ZOO TIME

Put an X to take away some animals, then write a subtraction equation to match.
Answers will vary.

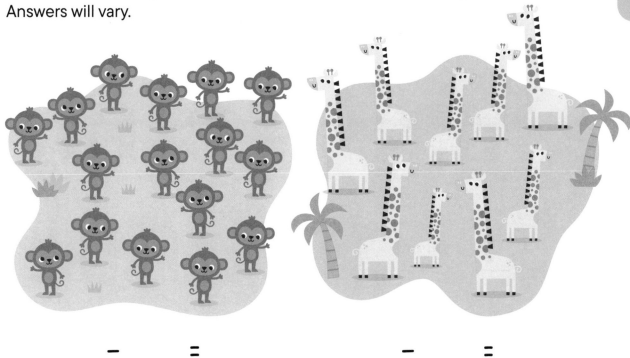

_____ – _____ = _____   _____ – _____ = _____

_____ – _____ = _____   _____ – _____ = _____

Activity 157

MAKE IT HAPPEN

Draw Os or Xs on the objects to make the addition or subtraction equation true.

4 + 9 = 13

13 - 8 = 5

5 + **7** = ____

12 + **6** = ____

17 - **9** = ____

20 - **12** = ____

Activity 158

NUMBERS GAME

Read the clues to find out the number. Use the number line to help.

0 1 2 3 4 5 6 7 8 9 10 11 12 13 14 15 16 17 18 19 20

I'm bigger than 5.

I'm smaller than 10.

I'm not the number 7.

Which numbers could I be?

I'm bigger than 10.

I'm smaller than 15.

I'm not the number 13.

Which numbers could I be?

_____

_____

Activity 159

ALIENS AWAY

Circle all the possible answers for the image of the alien ships.

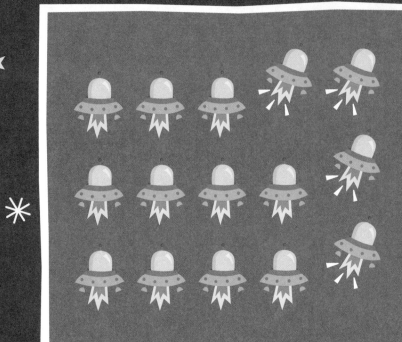

3 + 5 = 8

15 − 4 = 11

Eleven

15 − 11 = 4

Six

4 − 3 = 1

12 − 6 = 6

7 − 3 = 4

15 − 5 = 10

18 − 5 = 13

Ten

10 − 2 = 8

4 + 4 + 2 = 10

18 − 7 = 11

10 + 1 = 11

17 − 7 = 10

Activity 160
TRUE OR FALSE?

Read each equation. Write T if it is true. Write F if it is false. Explain to an adult why you think it is true or false. Draw pictures to help you explain.

True or False? _____

$5 + 5 = 6 + 4$

True or False? _____

$8 = 4 + 5$

HOW MANY HANDS?

Answer the questions using the handy chart below. If one hand has 5 fingers . . .

How many hands make 15 fingers? _____

How many hands make 30 fingers? _____

How many hands make 50 fingers? _____

How many hands make 100 fingers? _____

Activity 162

FILL THE EGG CARTON

Draw eggs in the carton and write an addition equation to match. Answers will vary.

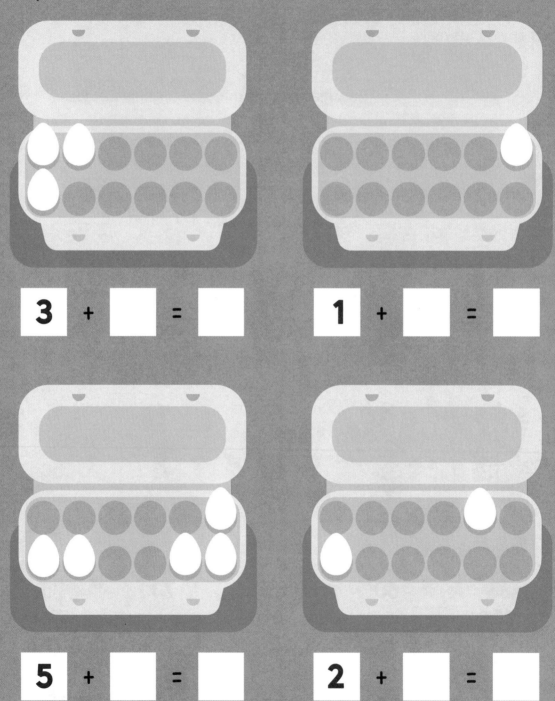

3 + ☐ = ☐ 1 + ☐ = ☐

5 + ☐ = ☐ 2 + ☐ = ☐

IS IT CORRECT?

Draw a picture for each problem to help you solve it and write the answer.
Explain to an adult how you got your answer.

Ashley said 2 cows have more feet than 3 chickens.
Is she right or wrong?   _____

Miles said there are more corners on 2 squares
than on 3 triangles. Is he right or wrong?   _____

Activity 164

WHAT NUMBER AM I?

Read the clues to find out the number. Use the number chart to help.

1	2	3	4	5	6	7	8	9	10
11	12	13	14	15	16	17	18	19	20
21	22	23	24	25	26	27	28	29	30

I'm bigger than 8.

I'm smaller than 15.

I have only one digit.

What number am I?

_____

I'm a two-digit number.

My number ends in 5.

I'm bigger than 20 but smaller than 30..

What number am I?

_____

Activity 165

WHAT DOESN'T BELONG?

Look at this group of four. Which one does not belong? Any of the four can be correct, as long as you explain why! Ask an adult if they agree with you.

Activity 166

TEAM PLAYERS

Solve the story problem. It has three parts.
Draw a picture to help you solve each problem and write the answer.

Coach has 17 players on his team.
9 players are hurt. How many players can play? _____

If 3 of the hurt players feel better and Coach says they can play,
now how many players can play? _____

How many players are still hurt? _____

Activity 167

MUSCLE CAR

Draw a picture for each problem to help you solve it and write the answer. Explain to an adult how you got your answer.

If one car has 4 wheels, how many cars make 20 wheels?   ———

How many cars make 40 wheels?   ———

Do you see a pattern?   Yes or No

Activity 168

ODD ONE OUT

Look at this group of four. Which one does not belong? Any of the four can be correct, as long as you explain why! Ask an adult if they agree with you.

TRUE OR FALSE?

Read each sentence. Write T if it is true. Write F if it is false. Explain to an adult why you think it is true or false. Draw pictures to help you explain.

5 is more than 3 + 3.

True or False? _____

8 is less than 10 – 1.

True or False? _____

10 is the same as 5 + 3 + 2.

True or False? _____

Activity 170

WHICH WINS?

Circle the group in each set that has more points.

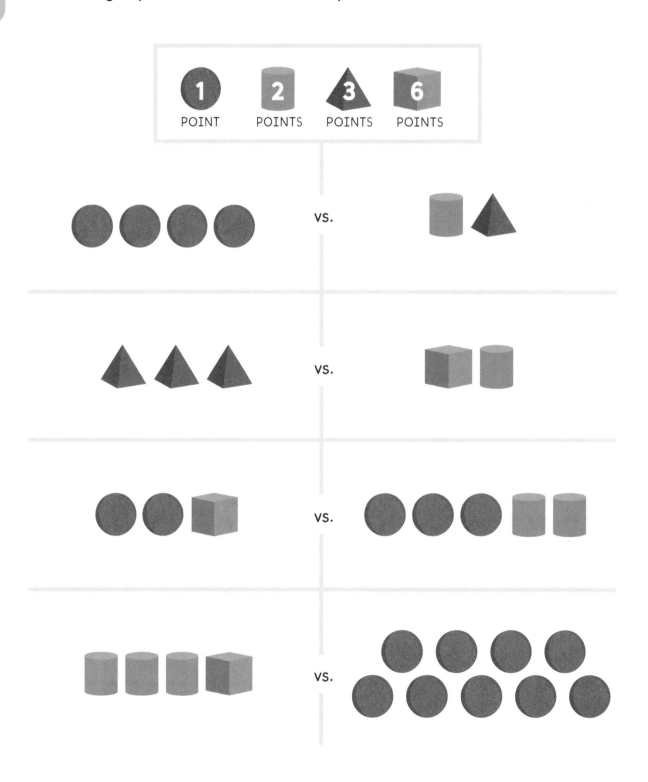

Activity 171

WHO IS RIGHT?

Read each problem and decide who is right.

Xander said 3 + 7 is more than 2 + 8.

Sydney said they are the same.

Who is right?   _____

Why?

Buddy said 10 + 5 is less than 20 – 2.

Lilo said 10 + 5 is more than 20 - 2.

Who is right?   _____

Why?

Activity 172

BALANCE THE SCALE

Draw the shapes on the scales that will add up to the same number of points.
Answers will vary.

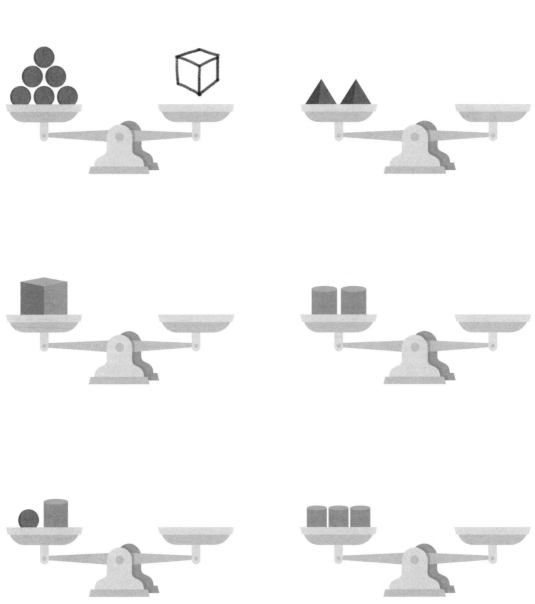

Activity 173

IS IT TRUE?

Read each equation and write T if it is true or F if it is false. Explain to an adult why you think it is true or false. Draw pictures to help you explain.

T or F?

$15 = 8 + 8$ _____

$4 - 4 = 0$ _____

6 is more than 2 + 3 _____

8 is the same as 4 + 4 _____

$8 - 5 = 4$ _____

Now make your own True or False question!

WOOF!

Activity 174

TREASURE HUNT

Help the pirate get to the treasure by answering the questions.

GOOD LUCK!

Where does the pirate go?	What **NUMBER** do you land on?	What **COLOR** do you land on?
You roll:		
Next you roll:		
Next you roll:		
Next you roll:		
Next you roll:		
Finally you roll:		

YAY!

Activity 175

TACO TIME

Order two sets of tacos using the numbers in the box, then solve your addition equations. Answers will vary.

| 7 | 9 | 13 | 15 | 5 | 3 | 11 | 8 | 2 |

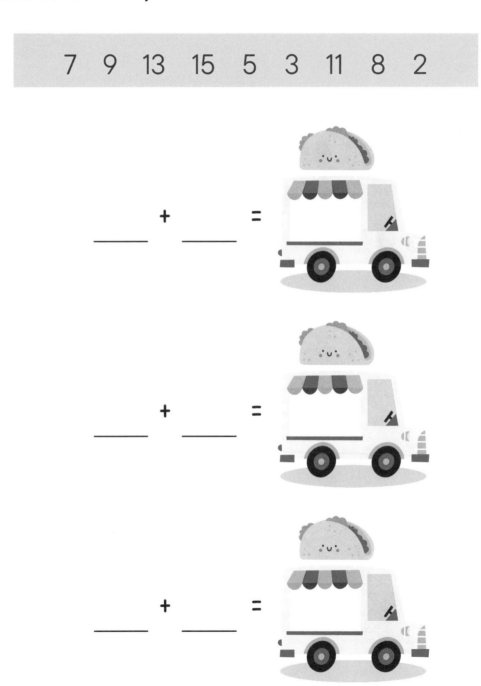

_____ + _____ =

_____ + _____ =

_____ + _____ =

ANSWER KEY

Some activities offer possible solutions and are marked "Answers will vary." Your child may have different answers throughout. Ask them why their answers do or don't work!

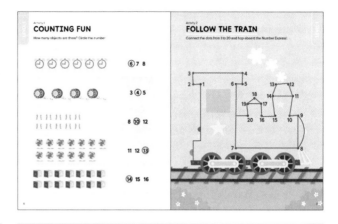

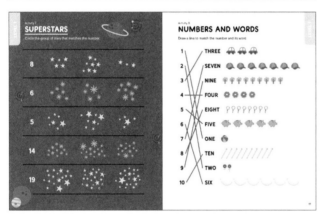

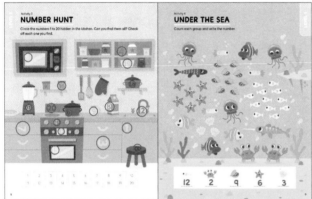

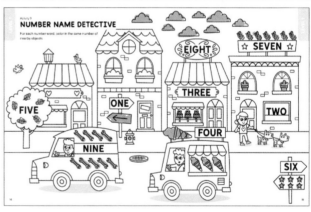

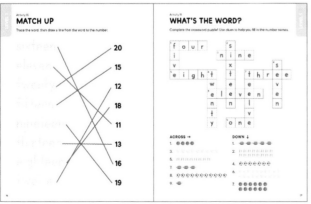

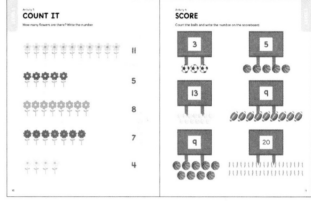

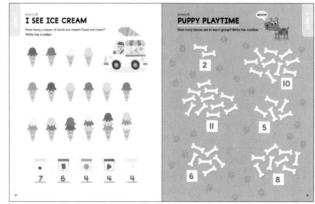

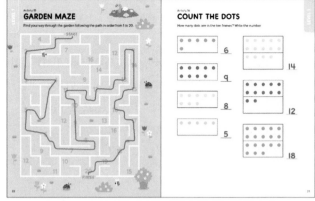

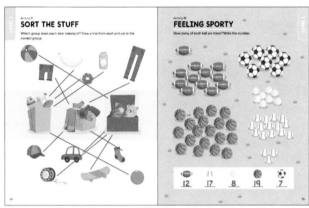

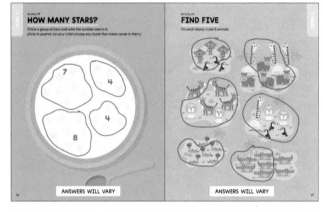

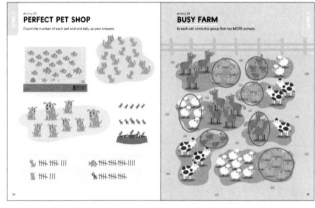

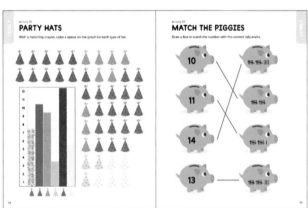

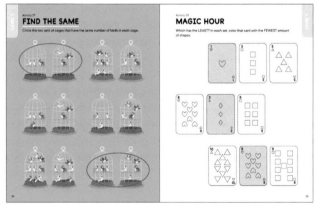

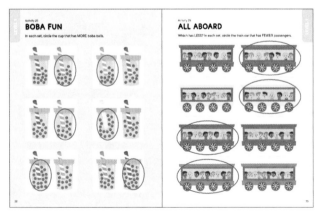

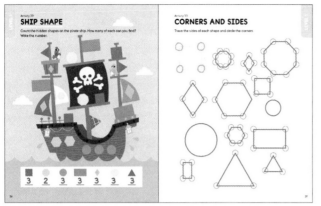

Activity 29
SHIP SHAPE
Count the hidden shapes on the pirate ship. How many of each can you find? Write the number.

3   2   3   3   3   3

Activity 30
CORNERS AND SIDES
Trace the sides of each shape and circle the corners.

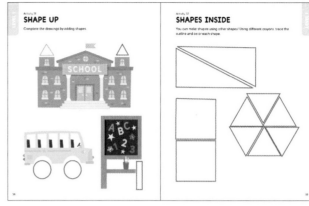

Activity 28
SHAPE UP
Complete the drawings by adding shapes.

Activity 27
SHAPES INSIDE
You can make shapes using other shapes! Using different crayons, trace the outline and color each shape.

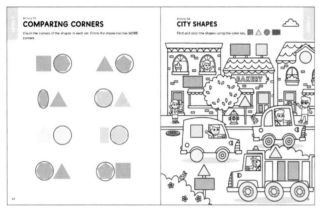

Activity 33
COMPARING CORNERS
Count the corners of the shapes in each set. Circle the shape that has MORE corners.

Activity 34
CITY SHAPES
Find and color the shapes using the color key.

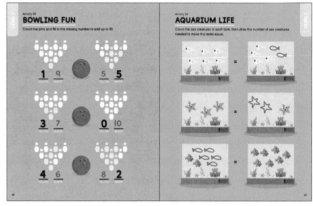

Activity 35
BOWLING FUN
Count the pins and fill in the missing number to add up to 10.

1   9   5   **5**

3   7   **0**   10

4   **6**   8   **2**

Activity 36
AQUARIUM LIFE
Count the sea creatures in each tank, then draw the number of sea creatures needed to make the tanks equal.

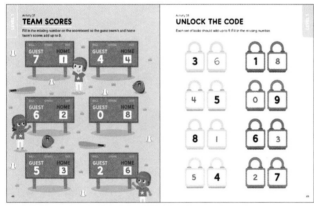

Activity 37
TEAM SCORES
Fill in the missing number on the scoreboard so the guest team's and home team's scores add up to 8.

GUEST 7   HOME **1**   GUEST 4   HOME **4**

GUEST 6   HOME **2**   GUEST 0   HOME **8**

GUEST 5   HOME **3**   GUEST 2   HOME **6**

Activity 38
UNLOCK THE CODE
Each set of locks should add up to 9. Fill in the missing number.

3   6   **1**   8

4   **5**   0   9

8   **1**   **6**   3

5   **4**   2   **7**

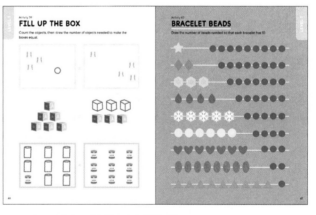

Activity 39
FILL UP THE BOX
Count the objects, then draw the number of objects needed to make the boxes equal.

Activity 40
BRACELET BEADS
Draw the number of beads needed so that each bracelet has 10.

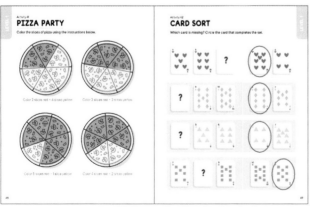

Activity 41
PIZZA PARTY
Color the slices of pizza using the instructions below.

Color 2 slices red + 4 slices yellow.

Color 3 slices red + 3 slices yellow.

Color 5 slices red + 1 slice yellow.

Color 4 slices red + 2 slices yellow.

Activity 42
CARD SORT
Which card is missing? Circle the card that completes the set.

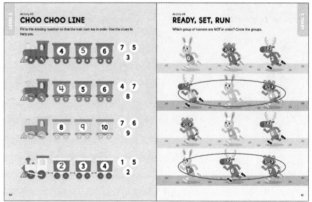

Activity 43
CHOO CHOO LINE
Fill in the missing number so that the train cars are in order. Use the clues to help you.

4 5 6   7 5 3

4 **5** 6   4 7 8

8 **9** 10   7 6 5

2 **3** 4   1 5 2

Activity 44
READY, SET, RUN
Which group of runners are NOT in order? Circle the groups.

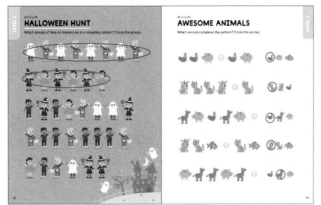

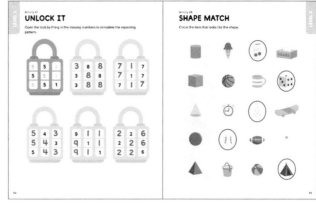

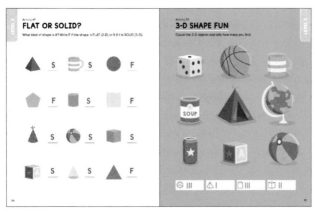

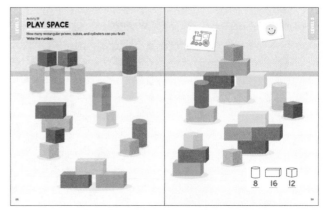

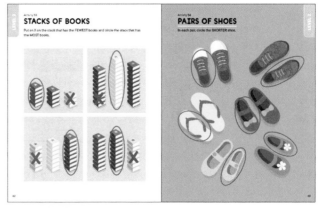

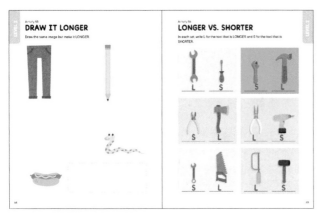

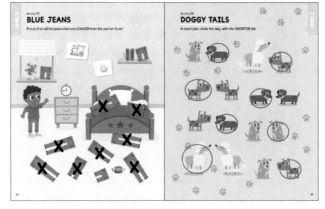

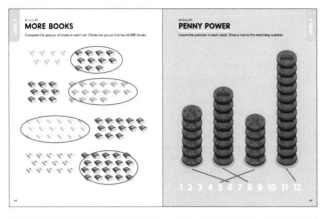

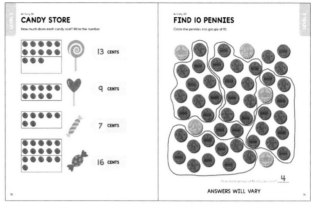

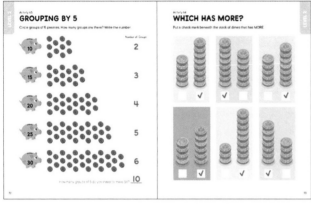

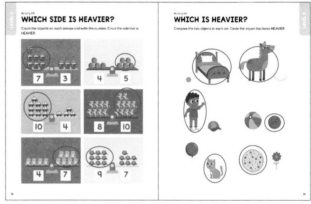

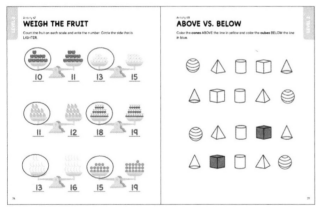

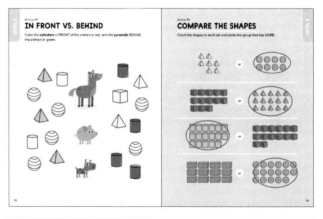

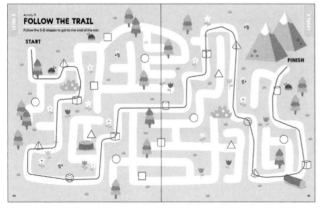

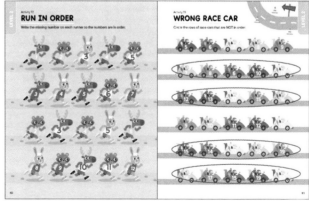

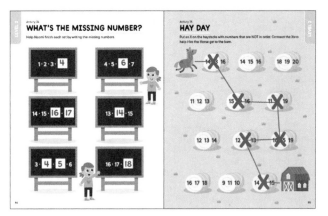

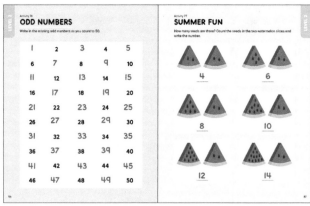

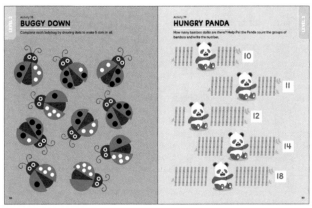

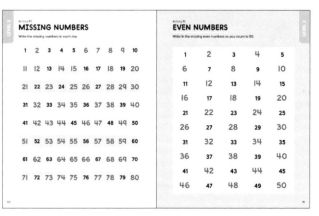

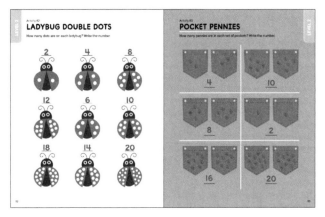

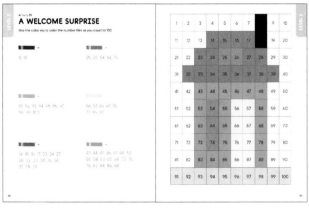

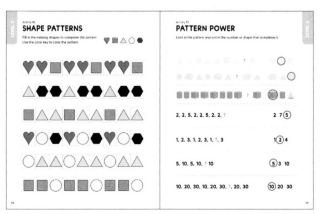

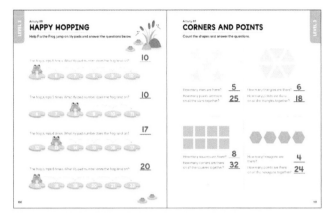

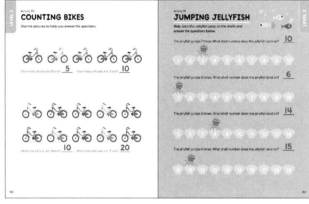

BY THE DOZEN / MAKE TWENTY

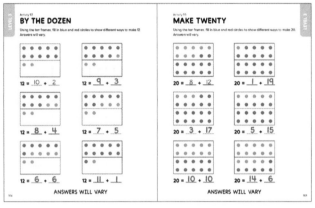

HAPPY HUNDRED

Activity 94 — Fill in the missing numbers as you count to 100.

1	2	3	4	5		6	7	8	9	10
11	12	13	14	15		16	17	18	19	20
21	22	23	24	25		26	27	28	29	30
31	32	33	34	35		36	37	38	39	40
41	42	43	44	45		46	47	48	49	50
51	52	53	54	55		56	57	58	59	60
61	62	63	64	65		66	67	68	69	70
71	72	73	74	75		76	77	78	79	80
81	82	83	84	85		86	87	88	89	90
91	92	93	94	95		96	97	98	99	100

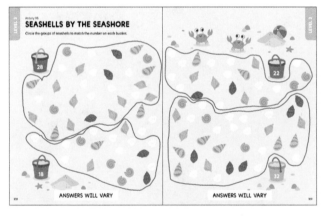

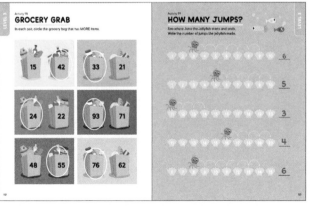

FIND 5s & Os

Activity 100 — Find and color every number that ends in 5 or 0.

1	2	3	4	5		6	7	8	9	10
11	12	13	14	15		16	17	18	19	20
21	22	23	24	25		26	27	28	29	30
31	32	33	34	35		36	37	38	39	40
41	42	43	44	45		46	47	48	49	50
51	52	53	54	55		56	57	58	59	60
61	62	63	64	65		66	67	68	69	70
71	72	73	74	75		76	77	78	79	80
81	82	83	84	85		86	87	88	89	90
91	92	93	94	95		96	97	98	99	100

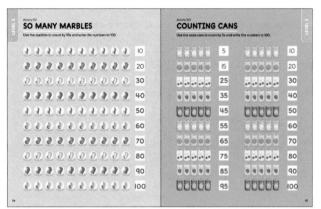

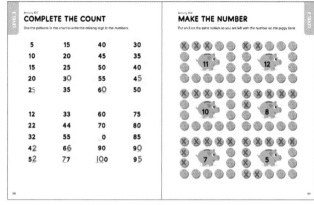

COMPLETE THE COUNT

Use the patterns in the chart to write the missing digit in the numbers.

5	15	40	30
10	20	45	35
15	25	50	40
20	30	55	45
25	35	60	50
12	33	60	75
22	44	70	80
32	55	0	85
42	66	90	90
52	77	100	95

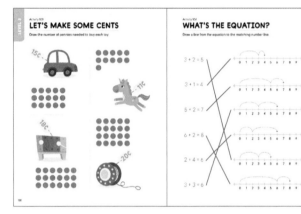

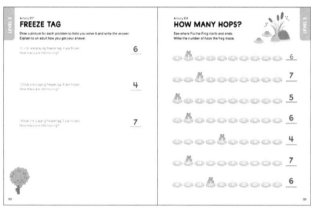

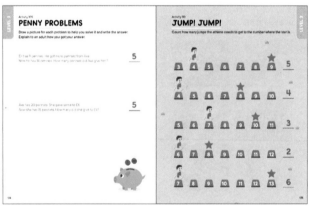

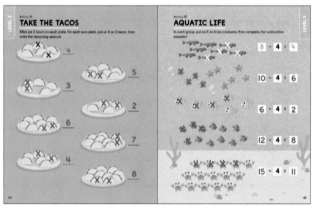

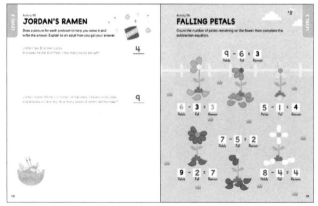

FRUIT BASKET

Count the fruit in each group and make an addition equation.

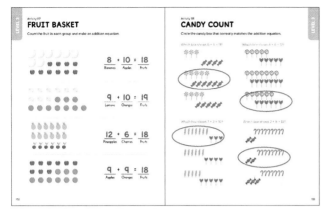

$8 + 10 = 18$
Bananas Apples Fruits

$9 + 10 = 19$
Lemons Oranges Fruits

$12 + 6 = 18$
Pineapples Cherries Fruits

$9 + 9 = 18$
Apples Oranges Fruits

CANDY COUNT

Circle the candy box that correctly matches the addition equation.

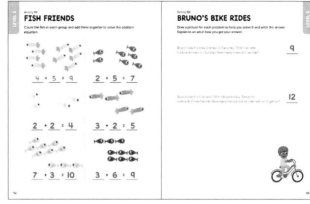

FISH FRIENDS

Count the fish in each group and add them together to solve the addition equation.

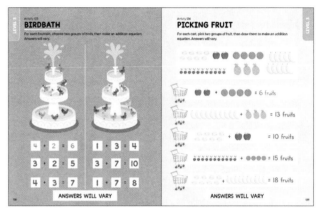

$4 + 5 = 9$ $2 + 5 = 7$

$2 + 2 = 4$ $3 + 2 = 5$

$7 + 3 = 10$ $3 + 6 = 9$

BRUNO'S BIKE RIDES

Draw a picture for each problem to help you solve it and write the answer. Explain to an adult how you got your answer.

Bruno rode his bike 3 times on Saturday. Then he rode his bike 6 times on Sunday. How many times did he ride? **9**

Bruno rode his bike with 5 friends yesterday. Today he rode with 7 new friends. How many friends did he ride with altogether? **12**

ADD ME UP

Complete the addition equations using the number lines.

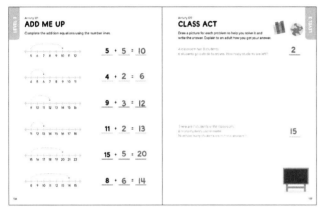

$5 + 5 = 10$

$4 + 2 = 6$

$9 + 3 = 12$

$11 + 2 = 13$

$15 + 5 = 20$

$8 + 6 = 14$

CLASS ACT

Draw a picture for each problem to help you solve it and write the answer. Explain to an adult how you got your answer.

A classroom has 8 students. 6 students go outside for recess. How many students are left? **2**

There are 7 students in the class pool. 8 more students come inside. How many students are in the classroom now? **15**

BIRDBATH

For each fountain, choose two groups of birds, then make an addition equation. Answers will vary.

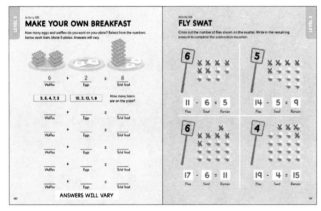

$4 + 2 = 6$ $1 + 3 = 4$

$3 + 2 = 5$ $3 + 7 = 10$

$4 + 3 = 7$ $1 + 7 = 8$

ANSWERS WILL VARY

PICKING FRUIT

For each cart, pick two groups of fruit, then draw them to make an addition equation. Answers will vary.

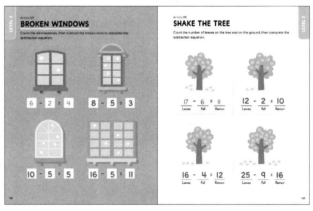

☐ + ●●●● = 6 fruits

☐ + ☐☐☐ = 13 fruits

☐ + ●● = 10 fruits

☐ + ●●●● = 15 fruits

☐ = 18 fruits

ANSWERS WILL VARY

MAKE YOUR OWN BREAKFAST

How many eggs and waffles do you want on your plate? Select from the numbers below each item. Make 5 plates. Answers will vary.

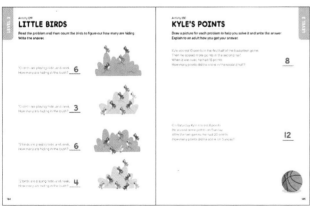

6 + 2 = 8
Waffles Eggs Total food

$5, 6, 4, 7, 3$ $10, 2, 12, 1, 8$ How many items are on the plate?

Waffles + Eggs = Total food

Waffles + Eggs = Total food

Waffles + Eggs = Total food

Waffles + Eggs = Total food

ANSWERS WILL VARY

FLY SWAT

Cross out the number of flies shown on the swatter. Write in the remaining amount to complete the subtraction equation.

$11 - 6 = 5$ $14 - 5 = 9$
Flies Swat Remain

$17 - 6 = 11$ $19 - 4 = 15$
Flies Swat Remain

BROKEN WINDOWS

Count the whole windows, then subtract the broken ones to complete the subtraction equation.

$6 - 2 = 4$ $8 - 5 = 3$

$10 - 5 = 5$ $16 - 5 = 11$

SHAKE THE TREE

Count the number of leaves on the tree and on the ground, then complete the subtraction equation.

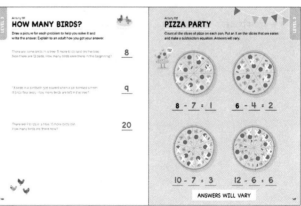

$17 - 6 = 11$ $12 - 2 = 10$
Leaves Fell Remain

$16 - 4 = 12$ $25 - 9 = 16$
Leaves Fell Remain

LITTLE BIRDS

Read the problem and then count the birds to figure out how many are hiding. Write the answer.

10 birds are playing hide and seek. How many are hiding in the bush? **6**

10 birds are playing hide and seek. How many are hiding in the bush? **3**

12 birds are playing hide and seek. How many are hiding in the bush? **6**

12 birds are playing hide and seek. How many are hiding in the bush? **4**

KYLE'S POINTS

Draw a picture for each problem to help you solve it and write the answer. Explain to an adult how you got your answer.

Kyle scored 10 points in the first half of the basketball game. Then he scored more points in the second half. When it was over, he had 18 points. How many points did he score in the second half? **8**

On Saturday Kyle scored 4 points. He scored some points on Sunday. After the two games, he had 16 points. How many points did he score on Sunday? **12**

HOW MANY BIRDS?

Draw a picture for each problem to help you solve it and write the answer.

There are some birds in a tree. 5 more birds land on the tree. Now there are 13 birds. How many birds were there in the beginning? **8**

13 birds in a birdbath got scared when a cat looked out. 4 birds flew away. How many birds are left in the tree? **9**

There are 9 birds in a tree. 11 more come too! How many birds are there now? **20**

PIZZA PARTY

Count all the slices of pizza on each pan. Put an X on the slices that are eaten and make a subtraction equation. Answers will vary.

$8 - 7 = 1$ $6 - 4 = 2$

$10 - 7 = 3$ $12 - 6 = 6$

ANSWERS WILL VARY

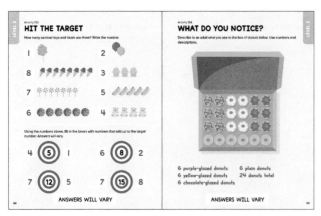

Activity 133
HIT THE TARGET
How many carnival toys and treats are there? Write the number.

1
2
8
3
7
5
6
4

Using the numbers above, fill in the boxes with numbers that add up to the target number. Answers will vary.

4 (5) 1 6 (8) 2
7 (12) 5 7 (15) 8

ANSWERS WILL VARY

Activity 134
WHAT DO YOU NOTICE?
Describe to an adult what you see in the box of donuts below. Use numbers and descriptions.

6 purple-glazed donuts
6 yellow-glazed donuts
6 chocolate-glazed donuts
6 plain donuts
24 donuts total

ANSWERS WILL VARY

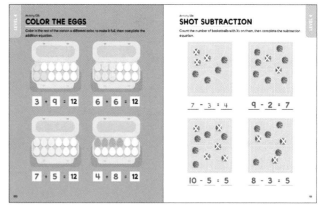

Activity 135
COLOR THE EGGS
Color in the rest of the carton a different color to make it full, then complete the addition equation.

$3 + 9 = 12$ $6 + 6 = 12$
$7 + 5 = 12$ $4 + 8 = 12$

Activity 136
SHOT SUBTRACTION
Count the number of basketballs with Xs on them, then complete the subtraction equation.

$7 - 3 = 4$ $9 - 2 = 7$
$10 - 5 = 5$ $8 - 3 = 5$

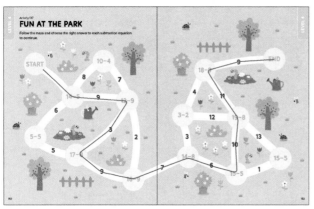

Activity 137
FUN AT THE PARK
Follow the maze and choose the right answer to each subtraction equation to continue.

Activity 138
KAYLIE'S SAND CRABS
Read each problem, then draw to solve and write the answer. Explain to an adult how you got your answer.

20
12
3

Activity 139
TRUE OR FALSE?
Write T if the sentence is true. Write F if it is false.

T
F
F
T
T

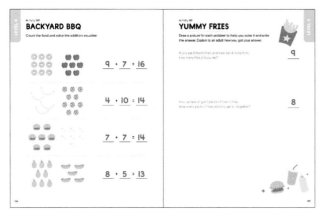

Activity 140
BACKYARD BBQ
Count the food and solve the addition equation.

$9 + 7 = 16$
$4 + 10 = 14$
$7 + 7 = 14$
$8 + 5 = 13$

Activity 141
YUMMY FRIES
Draw a picture for each problem to help you solve it and write the answer. Explain to an adult how you got your answer.

9
8

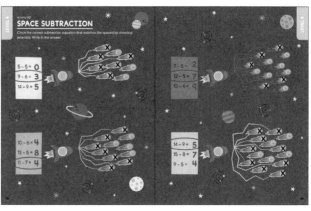

Activity 142
SPACE SUBTRACTION
Circle the correct subtraction equation that matches the spaceship shooting asteroids. Write in the answer.

$5 - 5 = 0$
$9 - 6 = 3$
$14 - 9 = 5$

$7 - 5 = 2$
$12 - 5 = 7$
$10 - 4 = 6$

$10 - 6 = 4$
$13 - 5 = 8$
$11 - 7 = 4$

$14 - 9 = 5$
$15 - 8 = 7$
$9 - 5 = 4$

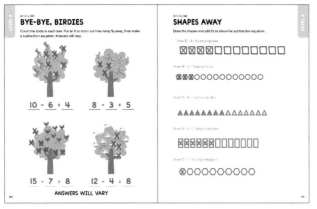

Activity 143
BYE-BYE, BIRDIES
Count the birds in each tree. Put an X to cross out how many fly away, then make a subtraction equation. Answers will vary.

$10 - 6 = 4$ $8 - 3 = 5$
$15 - 7 = 8$ $12 - 4 = 8$

ANSWERS WILL VARY

Activity 144
SHAPES AWAY
Draw the shapes and add Xs to show the subtraction equation.

Draw 10 - 4 = 6 using squares.
⊠⊠⊠⊠□□□□□□

Draw 14 - 3 = 11 using circles.
⊗⊗⊗○○○○○○○○○○○

Draw 15 - 8 = 7 using triangles.
▲▲▲▲▲▲▲▲△△△△△△△

Draw 13 - 6 = 7 using rectangles.
⊠⊠⊠⊠⊠⊠□□□□□□□

Draw 12 - 11 = 1 using hexagons.
⊗○○○○○○○○○○○

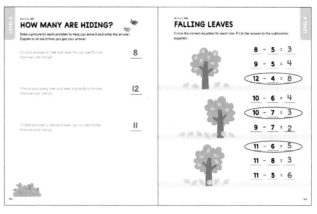

Activity 145
HOW MANY ARE HIDING?
Draw a picture for each problem to help you solve it and write the answer. Explain to an adult how you got your answer.

8
12
11

Activity 146
FALLING LEAVES
Circle the correct equation for each tree. Fill in the answer to the subtraction equation.

$8 - 5 = 3$
$9 - 5 = 4$
($12 - 4 = 8$)

$10 - 6 = 4$
($10 - 7 = 3$)
$9 - 7 = 2$

($11 - 6 = 5$)
$11 - 8 = 3$
$11 - 5 = 6$

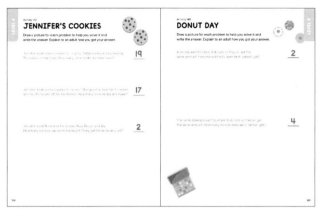

JENNIFER'S COOKIES

19

17

2

DONUT DAY

2

4

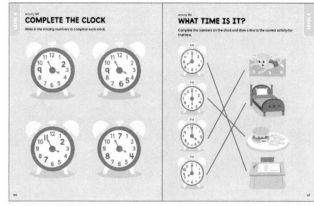

COMPLETE THE CLOCK

WHAT TIME IS IT?

AROUND THE CLOCK

READING MINUTES BY 5s

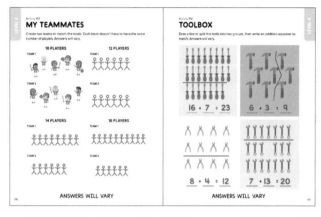

MY TEAMMATES

10 PLAYERS   12 PLAYERS

14 PLAYERS   16 PLAYERS

ANSWERS WILL VARY

TOOLBOX

$16 + 7 = 23$ $6 + 3 = 9$

$8 + 4 = 12$ $7 + 13 = 20$

ANSWERS WILL VARY

GONE FISHING

$12 - 4 = 8$ $6 - 3 = 3$

$10 - 7 = 3$ $12 - 2 = 10$

ANSWERS WILL VARY

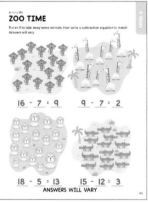

ZOO TIME

$16 - 7 = 9$ $9 - 7 = 2$

$18 - 5 = 13$ $15 - 12 = 3$

ANSWERS WILL VARY

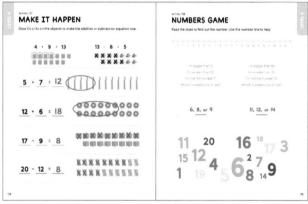

MAKE IT HAPPEN

$4 + 9 = 13$ $13 - 8 = 5$

$5 + 7 = 12$

$12 + 6 = 18$

$17 - 9 = 8$

$20 - 12 = 8$

NUMBERS GAME

6, 8, or 9   11, 12, or 14

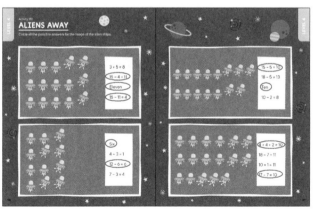

ALIENS AWAY

$3 + 5 = 8$
$15 - 4 = 11$
Eleven
$15 - 11 = 4$

$15 - 5 = 10$
$18 - 5 = 13$
Ten
$10 - 2 = 8$

Six
$4 - 3 = 1$
$12 - 6 = 6$
$7 - 3 = 4$

$4 + 4 + 2 = 10$
$18 - 7 = 12$
$10 + 1 = 11$
$17 - 7 = 10$

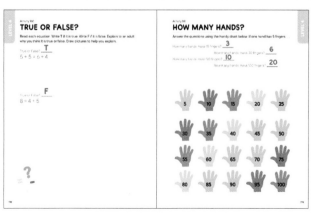

TRUE OR FALSE?

T
$5 + 5 = 6 + 4$

F
$8 = 4 + 5$

?

HOW MANY HANDS?

3

6

10

20

FILL THE EGG CARTON

Activity 162

Draw eggs in the carton and write an addition equation to match. Answers will vary.

$3 + 9 = 12$ $1 + 11 = 12$

$5 + 7 = 12$ $2 + 10 = 12$

ANSWERS WILL VARY

IS IT CORRECT?

Activity 163

Draw a picture for each problem to help you solve it and write the answer. Explain to an adult how you got your answer.

Ask an adult 2 cows have more feet than 3 chickens. Is she right or wrong?

right

Ashley is right because 2 cows have 8 feet, and 3 chickens have 6 feet.

Miles said there are more corners in 2 squares than on 3 triangles. Is he right or wrong?

wrong

Miles is wrong because 2 squares have 8 corners, and 3 triangles have 9 corners.

WHAT NUMBER AM I?

Activity 164

Read the clues to find out the number. Use the number chart to help.

1	2	3	4	5	6	7	8	9	10
11	12	13	14	15	16	17	18	19	20
21	22	23	24	25	26	27	28	29	30

I'm bigger than 8.
I'm smaller than 15.
I have only one digit.
What number am I?

9

I'm a two-digit number.
My number ends in 5.
I'm bigger than 20 but smaller than 30.
What number am I?

25

WHAT DOESN'T BELONG?

Activity 165

Look at this group of four. Which one does not belong? Any of the four can be correct, as long as you explain why! Ask an adult if they agree with you.

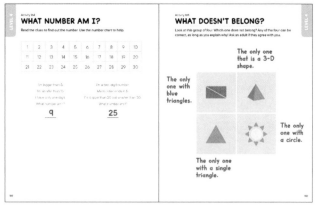

The only one with blue triangles.

The only one that is a 3-D shape.

The only one with a single triangle.

The only one with a circle.

TEAM PLAYERS

Activity 166

Solve this story problem. It has three parts.
Draw a picture to help you solve each problem and write the answer.

Coach has 17 players on his team.
9 players are hurt. How many players can play?

8

If 3 of the hurt players feel better and Coach says they can play, how many players can play?

11

How many players are still hurt?

6

MUSCLE CAR

Activity 167

Draw a picture for each problem to help you solve it and write the answer. Explain to an adult how you got your answer.

If one car has 4 wheels, how many cars make 20 wheels?

5

How many cars make 40 wheels?

10

Do you see a pattern?

(yes)

ODD ONE OUT

Activity 168

Look at this group of four. Which one does not belong? Any of the four can be correct, as long as you explain why! Ask an adult if they agree with you.

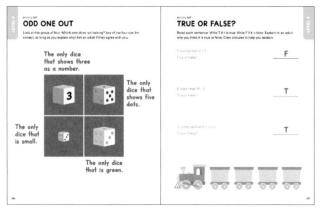

The only dice that shows three as a number.

The only dice that shows five dots.

The only dice that is small.

The only dice that is green.

TRUE OR FALSE?

Activity 169

Read each sentence. Write T if it is true or F if it is false. Explain to an adult why you think it is true or false. Draw pictures to help you explain.

5 is more than 3 + 3
True or False?

F

6 is less than 10 − 1
True or False?

T

12 is the same as 6 + 3 + 3
True or False?

T

WHICH WINS?

Activity 170

Circle the group in each set that has more points.

1	2		6
POINT	POINTS	POINTS	POINTS

4 ⬤⬤⬤⬤ vs (▲△ 5)

9 (▲▲▲) vs ◼◼ 8

8 (◼◼) vs ◼◼◼ 7

12 (◼◼◼) vs ⬤⬤⬤⬤ 9

WHO IS RIGHT?

Activity 171

Read each problem and decide who is right.

Xander said 3 + 10 is more than 3 + 8.
Sydney said they are the same.
Who is right?
Why?

Sydney

Both equations equal 10.

Buddy said 10 + 5 is more than 20 − 2.
Lola said 10 + 5 is less than 20 − 2.
Who is right?
Why?

Buddy

$10 + 5 = 15$, which is less than 18, and $20 − 2 = 18$.

BALANCE THE SCALE

Activity 172

Draw the shapes on the scales that add up to the same number of points. Answers will vary.

1	2		6
POINT	POINTS	POINTS	POINTS

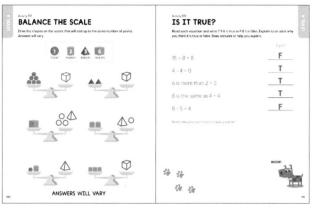

ANSWERS WILL VARY

IS IT TRUE?

Activity 173

Read each equation and write T if it is true or F if it is false. Explain to an adult why you think it is true or false. Draw pictures to help you explain.

T or F?

$15 = 8 + 8$ **F**

$4 − 4 = 0$ **T**

6 is more than 2 + 3 **T**

8 is the same as 4 + 4 **T**

$8 − 5 = 4$ **F**

Now make your own true or false question.

WOOF!

TREASURE HUNT

Activity 174

Help the pirate get to the treasure by answering the questions.

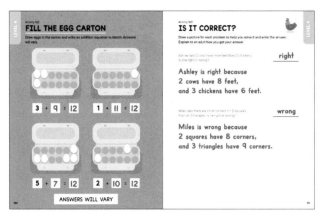

Where does the pirate go?	What NUMBER do you see?	What COLOR is it?
	5	Blue
	14	Yellow
	25	Blue
	33	Blue
	41	Blue
	50	Yellow

TACO TIME

Activity 175

Order two sets of tacos using the numbers in the box, then solve your addition equations. Answers will vary.

7 9 13 15 5 3 11 8 2

$9 + 15 = 24$

$5 + 11 = 16$

$7 + 5 = 15$

ANSWERS WILL VARY

206   ANSWER KEY

ABOUT THE AUTHOR

Naoya Imanishi, MEd, has been an educator in the Los Angeles Unified School District since 2000, serving as a third-grade teacher, math coach, and currently a school coordinator. He also works with the UCLA Mathematics Project as a teacher leader and coach for professional development in Cognitively Guided Instruction. While attaining his bachelor's and master's in education at UCLA, he was one of the first producers of LCC Theatre Company and co-founder of ProperGander, both Asian-American theatre companies with notable alumni. Naoya enjoys video editing and cooking for his wife, Jennifer, their two sons, Kyle and Jordan, and their dog, Buddy.

ABOUT THE ILLUSTRATOR

Gareth Williams lives in London with his amazing wife. From an early age he's loved to draw, and that passion continues to this day. It's something he still can't believe he gets to do for a living. Gareth's illustrated everything from editorial illustrations to children's books. He loved working on this project and hopes you will love it just as much.

Instagram: @gareth.designs

From board books to reads for teens, **Brightly** helps raise lifelong learners by celebrating the countless adventures and moments of connection that books can offer. We take pride in working with a diverse group of contributors, authors, and partners who provide a multitude of ways to cultivate a love of books and learning new skills in children of all ages.

A Brightly Book is expertly designed to provide young readers with a fun, age-appropriate, and hands-on learning experience. We hope you and your little ones enjoy this book as much as we do.

Happy reading!

See all that Brightly has to offer at **readbrightly.com**.